LIFELONG LEARNER

Reflections, Notes, Discoveries

MELISSA M. JOHNSON

LIFELONG LEARNER: REFLECTIONS, NOTES, DISCOVERIES

FIRST EDITION

ISBN: 979-8-9874199-6-0

Printed in the United States of America

BOOK DESIGN BY BRANCH CREATIVE CO.

MELISSA J CREATIVE

5015 S. WESTERN AVENUE, SUITE 290
SIOUX FALLS, SD 57108

MELISSAJCREATIVE.COM

PRAISE

for Lifelong Learner – Notes, Reflections, Discoveries

Melissa's latest book Lifelong Learner is a vulnerable journey through the life of a business owner, a parent of a child with exceptional needs, and an overcomer. Her storytelling will captivate you and cause you to reflect on your own life journey. I've known Melissa for two things: her resilience and her positivity. You'll find both in this amazing book!

JON GORDON *14-time Best-selling author of The Energy Bus and The Carpenter*

Reading Melissa's book – as a leader, a pastor, a mom, a woman, and a dreamer – I could feel the hope she brings through her words. Being all of those things in today's world can feel isolating. The adventure is beautifully scary. Melissa's words were a humanized companion. They were captivating.

It was a mix of self-improvement, continuing education, and storytelling. A rare gem in a sea of everyone's noisy ego. I instantly noted that it would be a book to have my leaders read. A different approach to church leadership. ***Not everything is strategic.*** Permission to jump out of the hamster wheel of keeping up with the world's empires.

Melissa is a force in our community. And with one brave sentence, she became relatable to every playing field: ***Sometimes staying alive is the bravest thing you can do.*** Melissa gives life in this powerful statement. The belief – in all of us – that there is hope to be found. Melissa claims to love words. This book is evidence. The pages had me stopping and staring. Wondering. Thinking. Imagining. Hoping... Several times I found myself yearning to share my own relatable story. Inspired. The words she loves are a gift to her readers. What a delight.

ERICA VARCOE *Founder, Pastor of The Table Ministry*

Lifelong Learner is a must-read! Melissa's honesty, vulnerability and reflection about her lifelong learning give you permission to be the same in your own journey. There are so many feelings I could relate to and so many things I learned because I am a lifelong learner too. It gives you a glimpse into her creative being while giving you permission to be more creative yourself. This book is a sweet companion that carries laughter and tears. It's like having candid conversations with a great friend that you don't want them to end.

PETRA KREBBS *Strengths Strategist ™ Petra Krebbs Consulting*

Melissa is a gifted writer. Every sentence I read puts me right in the moment with her and there were so many times I wanted to say, "me too!" She gets us and she ***is*** us. Her words are real so honest and true, not to mention enlightening and empowering. I would come back to this book again and again to be reminded of the golden nuggets she drops along the way.

JULIE NEE *VP of Training for the Jon Gordon Companies*

CONTENTS

DEDICATION

Dedicated to those who carry truths that are bigger, deeper, and more painful than any of us can imagine.

You are wild and you are brave.

INTRODUCTION
Say Anything

"Talk about anything. Whatever you're passionate about. Whatever you choose, we trust it will be great."

A few years back, I was asked to give a one-hour Zoom presentation to an audience of corporate women. When I meet with a client before a speaking engagement, I usually ask questions to determine what their theme is, what they'd like their audience to learn, or if they have an overall objective. But during this meeting, I was told I could speak on whatever I wanted women to know. I blinked at Jen and Dawn sitting across the table from me. I smiled blankly and tried not to have that "deer in the headlights" look, and blinked a few extra times. Anything I wanted to talk about? No objective? No theme? Nope. Just anything "We've seen you speak before, and we know that whatever you choose will be great."

It caused me to pause, reflect; what did I want people, especially women, to know? The question was so expansive, open ended. I went home from our meeting and deliberated. I thought about it as I sipped coffee the next morning on the wicker couch on my back porch. I kept thinking about it as I sat around the bonfire with my family that night. As Winne the Pooh would say, think, think, think, think, think.

And then that evening; my kids' end-of-school-year tradition: on the last day of every school year, they take all the past homework sheets they've collected and burn them. They throw everything into the flames and watch the page edges catch fire, curl, then turn black. Notebook covers bubble and peel away, pencil lead letters and numbers gradually fade into anonymity, and the flame eats away the evidence of their work until all that's left is a corroded, misshapen spiral notebook binding. To them, burning notebooks is a celebration marking the end of the school year and the hard work they put in. To me, it's disheartening. Scrawled fractions and history facts or not, I couldn't imagine throwing my notebooks into a fire and watching them burn away. I thought about my own piles of notebooks and journals collected in the house, every page filled with ink and thoughts and words. All the things I've jotted down when my mind was wandering and I was trying to keep it on track, or something a friend at coffee had said that I didn't want to forget. I thought of all the notes I've taken at conferences. I've always been an avid note-taker and so when I see a speaker, have a meeting with my team, sometimes even when I'm listening to a podcast, I've got a notebook nearby. As I reflected in front of the fire that night I thought, "Man, I really wish I could share all that good stuff with people. There's so much there."

The thoughts began to form through the gauzy smoke (which there was plenty of because no matter where I sit around a campfire the smoke always makes its way directly to me and my eyeballs and my lungs) and they came together into some kind of vague idea. *I think I want to share all these things I've learned from other people. These are things that I have found meaningful, and my guess is that other people would find them meaningful as well. I'd want to discuss books and conferences and I think I'd want to talk about the gifts of knowledge and wisdom and love that have been shared with me over time. I think I'd want to do sort of a "best of" all the things that I've picked up and found worthy of tucking into my pockets over the years and reaching in to grasp just when I need them most.*

The idea took shape, and eventually came to be the presentation I called, "Notes on Lives Well-Lived: The Things I've Learned from a Lifetime of Taking Notes." I had so much fun putting that talk together; more fun than I've ever had preparing a speaking engagement. I had notebooks scattered haphazardly across my kitchen island. They were filled with Post-It notes and index cards. Colored Sharpies littered the countertop, and my big white paper desk-pad was filled with doodles and disconnected words that all meant something to me. I arranged the presentation around six specific categories: notes on growth, leadership, success, fear, love, and legacy. I spent hours thumbing through my journals and my sparkly notebooks, doing my best to glean the good stuff.

I see great value in paying attention and taking notes. This habit has served me well through the years as I've been afforded the opportunity to hear many great speakers deliver on a variety of topics and I've referred to those notes many times. When I write things down, they soak in. And when I go back and revisit those notes, the brightest nuggets of wisdom gleam from the page.

This book is a compilation of those nuggets of wisdom I've collected. Some of it is so basic and simple, it's as obvious as getting hit alongside your head with a brick; you know it immediately and with certainty. But, before you roll your eyes and question why I'm even taking the time to share some of those simple truths, before you read a few sections and write the book off as a waste of your time, I have to wonder if, like me, you've found there are many things in life that are obvious like eating right, the benefits of exercise, the prudence of keeping a tight budget, etc. and yet sometimes we still need coaching or a little guidance to stay on track. Yep, some of the things I share are pretty simple, but I think they are worthy of revisiting.

Occasionally, I'll read something new or listen to a speaker or have a conversation with someone and I'm gifted with a gem that's about three levels beyond my current scope of understanding. Sometimes my mind is completely blown, and I've gained a new insight that totally changes my world. Why and how does that happen?

IT HAPPENS WHEN THE PEOPLE WHO'VE SHARED INSIGHT HAVE BEEN THROUGH A SITUATION THAT LENT THEM A DIFFERENT PERSPECTIVE THAN MINE. A PERSPECTIVE THEY ONLY COULD HAVE GAINED BY WALKING THROUGH FIRE AND COMING OUT ON THE OTHER SIDE.

These are the revolutionary tidbits that have changed my life in radical and positive ways. I believe they can do the same for you. I hope they do.

As such, I've arranged this book into four sections: The Discovery, The Learning, The Growing, and the Knowing. ***The Discovery*** is the first glimmer of understanding we might have about something within ourselves. When we start looking inward and trying to determine why we're here, and what we're about. ***The Learning*** is a two-fold section. Some of it is about the belief systems we have cultivated over time, and some of it is about questioning their validity. It's about taking what we have discovered and beginning to apply it to our lives. ***The Growing***—That's when we begin to build upon learning. It's inevitable for moving forward and becoming more than we are right now. Finally, ***The Knowing*** . . . well, that's the fun part. That's when we are so sure about something, we know it in the deepest parts of our soul and are unshakable in those beliefs. It's in the Knowing that we serve this world best.

I hope that by the end of this book, you'll be able to take some themes in your life and "level up." That you'll be able to identify things like self-confidence or your understanding of success or the directions of your passion and you'll be able to move from Learning, to Growing, to Knowing. That's where we are our most powerful in using the gifts God gave us. Use them. Grow with them. Know them.

· · · · · · · · · · ·

I gave my Zoom presentation *Things I've Learned from a Lifetime of Taking Notes* and even with some major tech difficulties (for example, I wasn't able to log in for my own presentation until eleven minutes after it was scheduled to begin. Yikes!) Even despite the challenges, I felt so good, so confident, because I was passionate about it. I shared the things I've learned that I'd want to share with my daughters or my best friend. I got great feedback and I still hear how one topic resonated with a person in a particular way or that something I touched on was what someone really needed to hear. The presentation was made up of other people's wisdom, but also of my own reflections and contemplations based upon the nuggets and notes I've picked up along the way.

Telling my friend Petra about it a few months later, she pointed out how much I came alive when talking about it.

You need to make that into a book.

You think so?

I worked that over in my mind for a few weeks, then months, and then I gave the same presentation again and I remembered how much it lit me up. Aside from Jesus' own teachings, these reflections are the stuff I have built my life on. Why wouldn't I want to share it in a more expanded form? So, I got to work.

THE RESEARCH

Dusting Off Old Notebooks

I might look like an adult, but my notebooks say I'm a twelve-year-old girl with a Kardashian's budget during school-supply season, because my notebooks have cheetah prints and sparkles on the front and I write my notes in any number of brightly colored pens. When I show up to take in a half-day workshop, I find the place in the room that has plenty of elbow room on either side of me, flip open my box of 24 colored gel pens, and I get to the good work of engaged listening. When the speaker changes or there's a topic shift or when I begin to lose focus, I switch pen colors. It keeps my notes fresh and you guys, they're vibrant and gorgeous.

Colored pens or typed pages, I wanted to give you these same nuggets of learning that have been shared with me over the years. I wish we could sit down together, you and me. I really want to grab a cup of coffee with you, sit down on the floor in my closet where most of my old notebooks are kept (which is a total mess, by the way so please just toss my boots to the side and find a bit of carpet to sit on.) I want to get cozy and look through my notebooks with you and be like, "Oh, this one! Yes! She was a great speaker. Ok, let me tell you about her. You know what I remember about her talk?" And then I'd recount the learning that has helped shape who I am. As I picture us discussing these things for hours, I'm overusing my hands to gesture wildly, and in my mind we are definitely wearing slippers so I hope you've got a good pair you love and I hope you wear them while you read the pages ahead. While you're at it, grab a blanket. Make yourself a cup of tea, if that's your thing, and get cozy.

I'm excited you are here with me. Please know that I'm honored to be gifted with the most precious resource you have, your time. Different from money or material possessions, time is the one thing we can't manufacture more of, and we can never get back. I don't take that lightly, so thank you in advance. Let this book take as much time or energy as makes sense to you. Find something that doesn't apply or resonate? Skip it! Promise I won't be mad, and the Book Police will not come knocking on your door and write you a yellow citation for improper reading practices. The cool thing is, you can pick up this book and read one or two passages in any order you choose. Choose what resonates with you when you pick it up. Some of the reflections are lighthearted and breezy, and some are deeper and will ask more of your heart. Choose whatever you're feeling and whatever you need.

There are going to be facets of me you'll discover on these pages that aren't usually public facing and they might surprise you. I'm not asking you to agree with everything I say, nor would I want you to. I'm only asking you to consider the words and thoughts, to reflect a little, and to see if these words open a new perspective or insight inside of you. As we enter the pages of this book together, I'm bringing my collection of lived experiences to the table and you're bringing yours, and they are undoubtedly a different set of experiences and histories. As my friend who is in AA always says, "take what you like and leave the rest."

When I began writing this book, I thought I had to be the expert. I thought I needed to share wisdom and package it in such a way that I could show you the clear path from hearing something for the first time (Point A) to the point where I applied it and then it changed my life for the better (Point B.) But some wisdom I haven't immediately applied to my life, no matter how great it is. Sometimes I circle around the same tree over and over before I get the strength or courage to actually climb.

That's me. That's my honesty. I'm still learning so much.

AS THE YEARS GO BY, I REALIZE THAT (SHOCKER!) I DON'T HAVE ALL THE ANSWERS AND I'VE STOPPED FEELING LIKE I'M SUPPOSED TO HAVE THEM.

I'm not the expert on anything. I'm stumbling through this messy world the same way you are. While I've come a long way from a time when I thought things were black and white, I don't have any of it figured out in this vast expanse of grey. Instead, I'm sharing some of the things I've absorbed and I'm challenging you to ask yourself some of the same questions I've considered. Examine your life closely enough and you'll find the answers that apply to you; the ones that resonate. The answers that deliver your *own personal brand of clarity.* I don't have the answers, but I can help you ask the right questions so you can discover the answers for yourself.

A LITTLE BIT AUDREY,
a Little Bit Amy

I was visiting the car wash a few weeks back. My car wasn't all that dirty, but I wanted the time in the tunnel of soap and water to clear my head. Driving through the car wash seems to not only rinse the dirt from my car, but also sweeps the cobwebs from my mind. I've recently learned I'm not the only one who seeks five minutes of peace and solace in the soapy dark tunnel of the carwash; a crazy number of people do this. Is this you, too? Do you find your peace among the suds? Wait, was that you in the blue Camry in front of me yesterday?

As I drove into the car wash that day a few weeks ago, the car wash worker who was spraying off my car waved at me and smiled, giving me a thumbs-up as he pointed to my license plate (CUPCAKE.) I chuckled and smiled back. He sprayed off my car and as the automation of the wash began to pull my car into the long tunnel, he tapped on my window again and mouthed a big "thank you!" What a personable guy. I tried to mouth back, "Thank you, too! I hope you have a great day!" but realized that my characteristic wordiness was pointless when trying to silently speak through the glass. Instead, I tried to use sign language to communicate my appreciation for his friendly demeanor. You guys, I'm not an American Sign Language expert; I don't know much more than a handful of basic signs. But my mom took some night classes in ASL when I was younger and my grandson can sign upwards of three words, so like, I don't want to brag, but I've picked up a few things here and there.

To make the sign for "thank you," you put the palm of your hand up to your mouth and then move it away in the direction of the other person. And so, I did. It was met with kind of a look of surprise mixed with confusion on Car Wash Man's face, followed by a pause. He held that look for just a beat before it became clear that he thought I had just blown him a kiss.

Slowly he smiled. And then he blew a kiss right back at me.

And I don't know how *you* do it, but that's how I end up blowing kisses in the carwash.

I'm a mess you guys; a whole, hot, mess of a girl who still thinks of myself as a girl but is likely seen by others as a middle-aged woman. I guess the fact that I'm a grandma probably means the *others* are right. But I'm a hot mess who is unapologetic and authentic. I'm capable of laughing at myself. In fact, more than capable, I'd say I'm particularly skilled at it. The comedienne Amy Poehler says, "There's power in looking silly and not caring that you do." I'm not saying I intentionally set out to look silly. No, usually, it's some haphazard misunderstanding like accidentally blowing kisses in the carwash. But I have learned that when I trip up the steps while walking onstage or I get uncontrollable, inappropriately timed giggles while interviewing a guest on the radio, (true story friends, it happened, and it was during a serious interview that was *not* a laughing matter) all I can do is laugh at myself instead of covering my face and hiding in embarrassment and shame. If I cowered and hid in embarrassment, I'd be buried so often my skin would grow pale and translucent like a creature of the night. I'd be a rosy-cheeked, pale-skinned, embarrassed vampire who would never see the light of day because they were perpetually terrified of their own awkwardness. And when I finally did come out of my cave, you wouldn't know if you should feel sorry for me or laugh at me, and even that would send me flailing and careening my way back into hiding. Brene Brown talks about getting into a shame spiral? Please. I'd be dangling precariously upside down in a shame cave of humiliation. Probably while having a wardrobe malfunction and clutching at my shoe and smearing my lipstick.

Yeah, I'm a little bit Audrey, a little bit Amy.

Audrey. Audrey Hepburn. Wasn't she something? She was the quintessential picture of elegance, grace, and understated beauty. Her chestnut brown hair spanned every style from a classic beehive to close-cropped and playful. Sometimes she wore a headscarf over her 'do, the edge of her cocoa-shaded tendrils peeking out along the front of the scarf and at the nape of her neck. Audrey's smile held an impetuousness that easily reached her eyes; eyes which were framed by thick, sculpted brows that were decades ahead of their time. Those eyes sparkled atop the delicate porcelain skin of her chin and cheeks. Waves of long lashes brushed the tops of those sculpted cheekbones as she'd avert her eyes demurely, a study in innocence mixed with undeniable allure. Audrey Hepburn was always impeccably dressed, and her keen sense of fashion is timeless. Audrey Hepburn not only *had* a certain aesthetic, but Audrey Hepburn *was* and *is* a whole aesthetic. *She's a whole vibe*, as the kids would say. Audrey lived her life with a coquettishness and an effervescence that could lift the weight of the world with just a giggle.

I'd like to think that, in some ways, I'm at least a little bit Audrey. But I'm also a little bit Amy.

As in, Amy Winehouse. She, on the other hand, was the freewheeling, eyeliner-sweeping engineer on the Hot Mess Express, someone whose most well-known musical hit was a song about people trying to convince her to go to rehab, but she said no, no, no. Her voice was oil and ashes, an aged velvet curtain in a smoke-filled jazz club. Tall, sinuous, and bony, Amy was someone who prioritized risk and adventure far above taking care of herself, a woman so talented and yet so hell-bent on living life with enormity that it ultimately led to her demise when she died tragically of an overdose. I long wondered what weighty suitcases full of trauma and agony Amy was clutching at her sides, dragging with her everywhere she went. I've always wondered what events and memories scarred her past that she found it necessary to numb it all in order to simply stay alive.

Whether Audrey or Amy, I think I've been a little bit of both.

Although, maybe instead of Audrey or Amy, I'm just me. Melissa. Maybe I'm not a picture of beauty and elegance, nor am I a wild- and winged-eyed creature who's running barefoot through hot coals down the path of self-destruction. Maybe I'm just me, doing the best I can with the tools I have in my back pocket. I think I'm finally beginning to accept that, as my friend Terryl once described me, I'm just "resilient, with grace," as authentic as I know how to be.

I'm authentic, and I'm glad. So glad and grateful that you're here, so that these words I've written aren't just going off into the void. I've written plenty of words in journals and notebooks that were *never* meant to reach another person's eyes and to be honest, I hope that when I'm gone, they will remain forever unseen, but I'm really glad you're here with me for these words. Because these words are special. They might get pretty raw. Some of them might be surprising. There are a fair number of words and stories in these pages that haven't been shared outside of my close circle of friends. So, I'm extending my arms and pulling you into that close circle with me in these pages, ok? The words have been penned just for you in hopes that you might see a little bit of Audrey, a little bit of Amy, a little bit of Melissa, and hopefully a little bit of *you* between these pages. If you were reading that last sentence and your inner jukebox just fired up Lou Bega's Mambo Number 5, that's totally fine and I get it. I'm with you, sister.

It is my sincere hope that this book is honest and authentic, and that it personifies my heart and my life's intentions. I've long wanted to write a book that helps people be open to discovering their own courage and truth. But as I said earlier, I don't have the keys to the secrets of life. Hell, I don't even have the keys to my car, and usually I've gotta stand in the parking lot balancing my phone and my coffee and my backpack, rummaging for my keys at the bottom of my purse. Hot mess, remember?

No, you won't find life's answers in the pages of this book. But I hope together we can walk a path that leads you down your own roads of understanding.

PART 1
The Discovery

Before the Learning, before the Growing, and way before the Knowing comes the Discovery. The Discovery is the first glimmer of self-awareness and curiosity that come into your periphery. The discovery is the fun part. The Discovery is the spark. The Discovery is the catalyst that ignites the magic of you.

THE PART WHERE THERE ARE WORDS FROM A WRITING EXPERT

Mentors come in many forms. I've had mentors in business, in my spiritual life, and on my personal journey. Some mentors are older, some are my peers, and some are on a very similar path I am on, only they might be a few steps ahead of me. Those mentors can help you because the things they've learned are so new, so fresh and recent, that it's natural to use them as a guidepost. Or in some cases, a sign warning you away from a path they've been down. Some mentors are an important part of a person's journey without even realizing it.

I consider Julia Cameron a creative mentor. Her work on cultivating and nourishing the creative being within each of us has inspired me and hundreds of thousands of other writers. Her Morning Pages method has revolutionized my waking routine and as a result, I've filled dozens of notebooks with my early-morning words. Her *Writer's Affirmations* from The Artist's Way have served as a code of conduct for me throughout my journey as a writer. When the writing has been painful, I've turned to number five. When I've questioned if the words I was penning were worthy of being seen by others, I've consulted number nine. Each of these affirmations has led me down the path of bringing these words to you and so here, I'm sharing that inspiration in hopes that they help inspire your creative being as well. I like to read these affirmations and rewrite them often. I like to ponder what each of them means to me as it seems the affirmation I need for any given day can change from the one I needed the day before last.

Read these affirmations with intention and love. Pull them into your heart and understand that creativity comes in many forms. For purposes of this chapter, I'm sharing Julia Cameron's Writer's Affirmations for someone committed to nurturing their inner creative writer. As you read, I hope you'll see yourself in them too, no matter what type of creativity you hold inside.

WRITER'S AFFIRMATIONS

from The Artist's Way by Julia Cameron

1. I am a channel for God's creativity, and my work comes to good.
2. My dreams come from God, and God has the power to accomplish them.
3. As I create and listen, I will be led.
4. Creativity is the Creator's will for me.
5. My creativity heals myself and others.
6. I am allowed to nurture my artist.
7. Through the use of a few simple tools, my creativity will flourish.
8. Through the use of my creativity, I serve God.
9. My creativity always leads me to truth and love.
10. My creativity leads me to forgiveness and to self-forgiveness.
11. There is a divine plan of goodness for me.
12. There is a divine plan of goodness for my work
13. As I listen to the Creator within, I am led.
14. As I listen to my creativity I am led to my creator.
15. I am willing to create.
16. I am willing to learn to let myself create.
17. I am willing to let God create through me.
18. I am willing to be of service through my creativity.
19. I am willing to experience my creative energy.
20. I am willing to use my creative talents.

NOTES ON CREATIVITY AND ART - OR- WHAT DO YOU WANT TO BE WHEN YOU GROW UP?

From the moment kids are in their first stages of verbal communication we ask them all the same question. We pat the on their cute little heads and we ask, "what do you want to be when you grow up?" The answer that a child can give to that question is based only upon their understanding of their miniature world, by the messages they've happened to absorb while watching the Disney Channel or Sesame Street, or what things they've gleaned from the six or so people around them, but we ask the question anyway. When my youngest daughter Lyric was little, she wanted to be a doctor. When my oldest daughter Randi was little, she wanted to be a fashion designer. When I was little, I wanted to be either an astronaut or a flower shop worker. The astronaut thing came from the movie Space Camp, which was highly popular when I was in elementary school. The flower shop worker, well, I'm guessing I saw an arranged bouquet somewhere and wanted to be the kind of person who created beauty. I believe the question "what do you want to be when you grow up?" is premature not only when kids are little, but at almost any age.

I like to paint. I like to make art. And even though I know better, *even though I know better*, I told someone the other day, "Well, I paint, but I'm not an artist or anything." I qualified myself, and then I immediately disqualified myself. Why? I don't know if you're like me, but I tend to base the validity of a thing on whether or not I'm getting paid for it. Messages around us continually tell us if we are not getting paid for something, we aren't really whatever that thing is. And so, we don't know what we want to be when we grow up because in many cases, we aren't getting paid to do the thing we love.

I write, but I'm not like, a real writer.

I bake, but I'm not really a baker.

I shoot photos on the weekends sometimes, but I'm not a real photographer.

I throw clay on the wheel whenever I get the opportunity but it's just a hobby, I'm not a potter.

Please stop that. Can I ask us all to please stop doing that? Please don't disqualify yourself by saying, "Oh, I'm not a writer," or "I'm not an artist. I'm really not all that creative." There. That word creative. That's the word that has caused thousands of painters to put away their brush and has caused many a poet to put down the pencil. We think that we aren't that creative and therefore there's no point in the pursuit. I think there are hundreds of thousands, maybe millions of people who aren't using their gifts because either someone told them they weren't good at it, or they aren't getting paid to do it. We believe we are lacking in creativity, so we stop doing the thing we love. Can I just tell you? You. Are. Creative.

There is creativity in everything you do. There is creativity in the way some accountants crunch numbers. There is creativity in the way a mechanic at an automotive shop uses a process and works through potential problems before arriving at the *actual problem* which then can lead her to the solution. There is creativity in the way a family plants a garden or makes meals or uses leftovers to build even more meals. If you've ever run kids to taekwondo or dance or band practice or soccer or school conferences, you'll know there is creativity in arranging everyone's schedule to ensure they arrive on time. You're a creative being simply by existing and navigating this world. Own that creativity, take pride in it.

As I said, I love to paint. And I have this painting that now hangs behind my desk in my office/writing studio. I love it now, but I didn't always. The canvas measures 5' wide by 4' tall. It's a big guy. And I've worked with and fussed over that canvas for years. When I started it, I remember the muted and bristly sound of my brush tapping forcefully against the canvas as I laid on clouds of vibrant yellows and sky blues that gradually led down to a deep and angry indigo, then a plum that faded into black. Tap, tap, tap. Bristle, step back, examine. Tap, tap,tap. Tilt my chin and wrinkle the side of my mouth. Tap, tap, tap. It was an expression of emotion: some days are bright and playful, other days are moody and dark. Sometimes the day can begin with one type of emotion, then fade into the other. I liked it. I hated it. It just wasn't quite right. It never felt like it was quite finished, so I put the canvas away for months.

This spring, I grabbed the canvas again from my art room and brought it out into the light. I dusted it off and decided it would be something completely different. The existing colors seemed too brash, too bold, and I needed to mute them a little. Instead of tapping my brush against the stretched canvas, I started making soft brushstrokes side to side, then up and down. Pale portrait pink. A Tuscan yellow gold. Dusty light sage. A crosshatch of an off-white color called parchment. Brush stroke after brush stroke, I covered up the vibrant hues that lived on the stretched fabric. I stepped back, considered. Scrunched up the side of my mouth again.

I had been going for *subdued*, but now it just looked old, antique, tired. Instead of giving a feeling of calm, it looked lifeless and sedate. It needed something more: flowers. Yes, I would make some abstract, flower-ish shapes. So, I laid portrait pink and a marine green onto the canvas, rounding out the abstract flowers and painting myself a garden. I liked it for a bit, but my scale was way off. I had painted a Gulliver's Travels-esque landscape of Lilliputian and Brobdingnagian proportions: both enormous flowers and miniscule flowers sharing space next to one another on the big painted rectangle. Ugh. I mean, it could be kind of ok? Parts of me liked it. Most of me hated it.

I put it away again for a few months, then hauled it back out of hiding. It still wasn't right. I covered up the disproportionate flowers with brushstrokes of pure white, all of them in varying sizes. I let it dry for a few days and I left it out where I could see it. I walked past it intermittently, scrunched up my face with curiosity and consideration, and kept walking.

In late May, my son Brandon tested the strength of his wings, found them strong and sure, and moved out on his own. And historically, when I'm going through a period of both mourning what was and celebrating what *is*, I paint. It doesn't matter what I'm painting, but that's my method of processing. This time instead of canvas, I painted the walls in his bedroom. The walls that I had painted racecar red and grey back when he still shared his bed with his stuffed animals were now a bright and cheerful white filled with air and possibility. The room glows, the light pours in and bounces off the walls, and I can breathe when I'm in this place. I moved a modern, clean white desk and some plants into the space, and a twin bed with bedding the color of pale cherry blossoms into the corner. I hung a vision board. It was quickly becoming my office, my writing studio, a space of my own.

Then I got Covid, and I was forced to stay home and get really quiet. I loved the new little space I had created, so even while I was sick, I spent a lot of time in it. When my body was tired, I napped on the nap nook in the corner. When I had a little energy, I found myself working on that canvas. Over the white I brushed on some pale blue green, ballet slipper pink, and the most magical, fairytale lavender. I began using my brush to dab gently this time, not tapping so forcefully, and I let the paint show me where it wanted to go.

I dabbed some ovals of white over some of the ovals of color, letting the layers of pink and teal blue and pale purple play together and stack on top of one another. I added in some gold and some streaks of iridescent glitter. It felt easy, joyful. I had been forcing the paint before, but now I was breathing, letting it play, letting the paint itself decide. I worked on that canvas all throughout my sickness, and when I was finished, I had a painting that had developed to be more authentically *me* than anything I've painted before or since. It felt like an act of creative defiance in the face of my illness, and also in the face of some other difficult situations I was working through that week. After literally years of trying to force this painting to be something it wasn't comfortable being, the painting itself had finally decided what it wanted to be.

That painting is such a metaphor for us as individuals. We just don't know what we want to be when we grow up. And we try on different colors and personalities and try to make them fit, many times based upon the expectations of the people around us. In middle school, I was trying to be seen, stand out, and I thought I needed to be loud, bold, and have a smartass answer to every question or statement to hold someone's attention. As a young mom, I thought I needed to cut my hair to a tasteful shoulder-length bob and wear sensible shoes and dress my girls adorably in coordinating outfits and colors. I loved doing it, sure, but I also felt it was an expectation so people would know I was a good mom. As I grew older, I looked at some of the black concert t-shirts I was still wearing once in a while and I decided that wasn't what a mature adult would wear, so I started shopping at other stores with lighter colored threads. I covered up "concert t-shirt girl" with something quieter, more acceptable. (Read: boring.)

Now? After all this time I've stopped pushing life so much. No longer do I forcefully *tap*, *tap*, *tap* my brush onto the canvas. No longer do I work so hard to try to fit into a box. I still fall on old patterns and sometimes find myself shapeshifting into whoever I'm expected to be by those around me. But when those old patterns and habits emerge like a part of the canvas that hasn't gotten covered quite yet, I'm quicker to forgive myself for the times I still try to fit into the mold of others' expectations. Instead, most of the time now I attempt to hold myself to my *own* expectations. Some days I'm still deciding who I'm going to be. But mostly now, mostly I'm just letting the paint flow onto the canvas and do what it wants. As I age, different colors are layering on top of others, and that's totally ok with me. There are layers that are both vibrant and loud, and layers that are quieter and more subdued. I'm noticing more substance to each of those varied layers. Patterns are emerging, things are taking shape, and much like that canvas finally deciding what it wanted to become, I'm getting closer and closer to that feeling of "deciding what I want to be" every day.

I challenge you to think about and discover all the ways you use creativity in your life. Remember, just because you aren't getting paid for your (art, music, writing, kid-chauffeuring) doesn't mean you aren't that thing. Own that title; be proud of your creativity. Let go of expectation and let the painting of your life take shape with ease. Discover what's underneath and discover what you're still becoming. Pursue the things that bring you joy and let your life decide what it wants to become.

REFLECTION QUESTION: *If you were to create a painting of your life, what colors would you brush onto the canvas? How would you describe your brush strokes? How can you go about discovering how your canvas will develop?*

NOTES ON VALUES

In my first book I spent a whole chapter talking about values. They are one of my favorite topics to talk about and write about and think about. But lately I've been reflecting a little more deeply, and I confess I'm a little puzzled by the origin of values. Here's how this will work: I'm going to write, and you'll read my words as they come out, and hopefully by the end of this section we both will have figured out what our values are and how we came to identify with them.

I think values are the hill you plant your flag on and claim as your own. Values are the ground beneath your feet and the foundation you construct your life on. Every decision you make is decided one way or another because of a value you cling to tightly and with passion. Webster's dictionary describes values as *a person's principles or standards of behavior; one's judgement of what's important in life.* And while yes, I'm clear on what values are, I've started to question where our values come from. I mean, I thought they were mine. But how did I come to see these things as my own principles or standards? What made me decide that these were the principles I wanted to live by?

When we are born, we learn the rules of the family systems around us. We learn what is seen as right or wrong in the eyes of the ones we love. We learn what is acceptable and when we're pushing boundaries, we learn how far is too far. Through subtle programming, we come to know what things to be proud of and which things we should feel shame about. Our conditioning is molded and shaped by the unspoken code of the village around us.

As a child I learned that being seen and not heard was perfectly acceptable and encouraged, but to be loud and messy meant I was being "too much." Values I'd associate with this conditioning include (but are definitely not limited to) obedience, respect, and accountability.

And by watching my mom smile through her tears, watching her always find the best in a situation, and watching her rush to laugh and make a lighthearted joke when someone tried to get too close to the root of any pain she was carrying, I came to believe that was expected of me as well. I'm quite certain that, based on my own upbringing and for better or for worse, I raised my girls to be the same. Capable. Resilient. Concerned for others. Strong.

Each of those words are values, certainly. But unwittingly, I think I learned a way of living and passed it down to my daughters. I taught them to be something else: I taught them to be quiet. To say everything was, "fine, just fine," when in reality, things are sometimes far from fine. The values I learned became the values I taught: they became my own, and then my children's standards of behavior.

So, when I identify my own values and tell you what they are (integrity, generosity, commitment to family, and joy) I'm beginning to question where those values come from. These are things that are important, but who told me those things were important to me? How did I identify that those were the foundation I wanted to grow my life on, the guideposts I would make decisions on? How did I come to know that each of those were the hill I wanted to die on, to stake my flag and say, *above all else, these are the things worth fighting for?*

My hunch? My hunch is that as we grow into our own people with our own thoughts, we begin to notice behaviors in other people. Not just within our family systems, but far beyond as well. At least for me, I think I started to pay attention to people I admired and I watched how they acted, how they made decisions, and how they lived their lives. I can think of tons of people who shaped me: one of my first bosses, Doug Van Zee, the owner of the grocery store I worked in, who would come out of his office and step away from his important work to sack groceries when we got busy. Why? Because he knew that without satisfied customers or hardworking checkers, he wouldn't have any important work to do. From him I learned servant leadership and humility. No job was beneath him; everything and everyone mattered.

A few years after working at that grocery store, my budding entrepreneurial spirit led me to take a study-at-home course to become a certified balloon artist (it's a thing.) My old boss Doug hired me to do a balloon arch back by the store's flower shop for Mother's Day weekend. I constructed this great balloon arch made of pink and yellow and white balloons at the end of the aisle leading to the floral department on a Thursday evening as the store closed. Despite my best efforts, I was devastated to find that by Friday morning, that balloon arch was beginning to fall, bobbing halfheartedly across the aisle, more of a nuisance to push out of the way than an arch of celebration overhead. By Friday afternoon, the balloon arch failed miserably, fell, and became more like a balloon hurdle to step over as you tried to pass through the aisle. I was mortified. I was just twenty years old and of course, brand new to the business world. I had quoted him a price that seemed exorbitant to me but in reality, barely covered my costs and time. And my project had failed. I apologized and told him that obviously he didn't have to pay me. I didn't deliver on what he had asked for or what I had promised. I'll never forget Doug grabbing the store checkbook and saying, "I hired you to do the work. You did the work. *There's value in the effort.*"

I'll never forget the grace I felt as he handed me that check; full payment for the work I had done. I vowed to do better, as much for my own pride as for wanting to make him proud. He gave me consideration and recognized the effort, even if the result wasn't what I wanted it to be. I'll never forget how he insisted on paying me for the value of the attempt rather than for the result. Values I learned from Doug: *Humility. Grace. Belief. Integrity. Work ethic.*

A few years later when I was gleefully expecting my firstborn Randi, I worked at a maternity store. My boss Debbie was from California, a transplant to our state, and I watched as she treated everyone with respect, but didn't allow anyone to walk over her, either. I listened to the way she spoke. I paid attention to her turns of phrase. My small-town upbringing meant I didn't make use of the most sophisticated language. But she did, and I quietly watched her. I listened. I learned. I looked up to her as a businesswoman. She gave me more responsibility than I'd ever been given before, and I took my duties seriously. She believed in me, and I started to believe in myself. Some of the values I learned from Debbie: *Confidence. Competence. Resilience. Empowerment.*

I have had so many people cross my path over the years who have taught me things without them even knowing it. I'm an observer and I pick up little things from every conversation and every interaction. Whether that's good or bad, it is a thing I do. Some people have taught me about the things I value and what I want to be, and others have taught me what I do not want to become no matter what.

I had a boss years ago in radio who asked me to forge winner names on a contest log sheet. The conversation went something like this:

Just write some names in, doesn't matter who you put or what their names are. We just have to send it into the organization and let them know we gave away their prizes.

But, if I'm making up names, then I'm not writing down the names of people who actually won.

It doesn't matter. It's no big deal. Just fill it out and fax it off when you're done.

I remember that day. I sat there, incredulous at what I had just been asked to do: forge names, even make up fake names, and send to the organization who would take us at our word that these were the winners of the contest we had agreed to run on our station. It was a flat lie, and I was being asked to hold the pen and write it.

I waited for a few minutes, trying to figure out what to do. I stared at the sheets in front of me, all white space and black lines. I gathered them up and took a deep breath. I found my boss in his office and said, "I can't fill these out. I'm sorry, I just can't." I laid them on his desk and walked out without any further discussion. I don't know what happened to those prize sheets. I imagine he filled them out himself and faxed them in. We never discussed it again and wrath did not come down upon me like I had worried it would if I took a stand.

But I learned something about myself that day. Young, partying, and working at a rock radio station, I think I surprised myself a little when I learned how fundamentally necessary it was to me to do the right thing. Did that passion well up solely because of the way I was raised? Probably had something to do with it. But it was more than that: it was stronger, more personal. I came to claim that value as my own once I recognized how deeply its resonance split down the center of my chest, how it bubbled up from inside of me not only because of external influences, but from deep inside my very existence. It felt good to do the right thing. It was liberating. And even though I didn't have the right words to describe exactly what I was feeling in that moment, that feeling is what I have come to know as integrity.

That feeling of liberation and resonance is how I have identified and grown my life's own personal values. I've paid close attention to instinctual responses when they bubble up, and I've gotten curious about where they're coming from. When something reaches me on that deeply personal level, I've come to recognize that feeling as my own and not just a result of any prior conditioning. Integrity is one of my own core values.

I can't decide which values ring true for you; the things that resonate so deeply within you that you'd fight for them with all you have might be different for you than they are for me.

VALUES ARE DEARLY HELD TREASURES THAT YOU DISCOVER, UNCOVER, AND DECIDE ON YOUR OWN.

Our shared values bind us together and give us a commonality, but our differing values bring color and variety to our world. They create an entire landscape of people who are passionate about the things they believe in, giving our world texture and depth.

Sometimes you'll discover a value when you're faced with a specific situation like I was, and your reaction will reveal something you didn't even know was locked inside. But another way to discover them is to look up a list of values and start sifting through them. I've got an extensive list in my first book, and I've included an even more comprehensive list in the appendix of this book. As you read them and sort through them, keep a dictionary nearby, or at least Google, which, handily enough, is nearby every second of our lives. If there is a word whose meaning you aren't quite sure of, take the time to look it up. When you read a description to a word, consider how it resonates with you and how it feels deep in your gut. That process of digging through, unearthing what's inside is a worthy pursuit in and of itself. Plus, who doesn't love to pore over gorgeous words?

I recommend pulling out ten, or fifteen words that resonate with you. Write them down. Really think about what each of them means. Do any of the words carry similar meanings? And if so, which one would you choose if you had to choose one over the other?

After you've written them down and examined them well, narrow your list to five. You have to get rid of all the rest. Really? Yeah. Sorry. You can't keep them all. I'm moving you towards a place where you'll engage with your clarity, and having more than five words will muddy the waters. Five. That's what you get. You there? How do those feel?

Ok, but slow down a second. There's an important distinction I want you to sort through: Have you chosen words that ring true to the depths of your heart? Or have you chosen words you think are expected of you? Remember, we are all told from a young age what and how and who we are supposed to be. Unearthing your own values is about you discovering the ways you want to interact with the world around you. My dear coach Shelli talks about "the ways you want to be in the world" and something about that phrasing helps me narrow down the list each time I go over it. This list of values you're creating is about identifying the impact you want to leave on the people around you; the ways you hope to engage with humanity.

Now we're going to pare our list down again. See if you can take away two more, get down to a list of three values. Just three. I like things in threes. Threes are easier to remember than five. For example, I'm a big fan of the Strengthsfinder test. And I know my top five strengths as identified by my test results but when I'm trying to tell someone what they are, I find myself inevitably having to fumble around to remember a couple of them, and I certainly can't remember which order they are in.

Trust me on this: choose just three values. Three is concise. Three is easy. Three is clean. Identifying just three values is an act of engaging with your sharpest clarity. Get your list down to three, then follow them, filter with them, and find peace with them.

REFLECTION: *May I not only discover and decide what my core values are, but may I make a conscious effort to live by them each day. When I make decisions about the important things in life, may I consult my list of core values as my guide.*

NOTES ON RENTED THOUGHTS - OR - HOW MUCH DOES THIS BELIEF COST?

"I am the wisest man alive, for I know one thing: and that is that I know nothing." – Socrates

Have you ever just been cruising along through your day and had a thought pop into your head and wondered where it came from? I mean like a really strong thought; one that leads you to a feeling or a belief about someone. While we aren't always aware of our thoughts, sometimes we catch a thought and realize that it was borne of messages we heard long ago. The first time that conscious awareness hit me, I got curious about where it came from. It was a particularly strong thought about someone, and when I stopped to examine it, I realized it wasn't rooted in any sort of truth but rooted in something that I was told long ago. This time I realized that the thought wasn't mine after all; I had *rented* it from someone else.

At some time in your life, you might realize you've been renting your thoughts from someone else. You might have originally rented a thought from your parents, your friends, religious leaders, the media, or heck, even someone you met one time that looked like they had things all figured out. My guess is that they didn't have their shit together any more than the rest of us do.

But for each of us, there comes a time when you discover that your thoughts about a situation or a topic or even about certain people have been rented; the thoughts aren't owned by you, but by someone else. Make no mistake, when you rent someone else's thoughts instead of owning your own, there is a cost associated with letting someone else tell you what to think and believe.

Wait. Do I really believe this? Or have I been conditioned to believe it by the people around me? Just because someone leads you to believe something doesn't mean a thought is owned by you.

Most everyone begins their life by renting a place instead of owning, right? But after a while as we age and grow and mature, we discover that owning is best. Once you've decided to own a thought, it becomes yours. You might examine a thought and decide you like the street where this thought lives and the neighborhood suits you and you have no interest in moving. You might keep the same thought you've been renting your whole life. And that's totally cool, too!

THE IMPORTANT THING IS THAT YOU DECIDE FOR YOURSELF.

When I first recognized that some of my beliefs weren't actually mine, it was deeply upsetting because, well, first of all, I wondered how many other things in my life I had been sold and told and just picked up without question. It set my world a little off kilter to realize I had different thoughts about something or someone than the ones I had spent my lifetime with. And I felt like the people I had been renting my thoughts from had moved into my consciousness without me even knowing it. I felt like they were literally camping out in my head without permission like some uninvited, ungrateful squatter. But over time I have come to understand that it's not like that: the other person isn't renting space in my head, but rather I am spending my energy renting the *thoughts* that they owned and passed on to me.

Maybe you were told that cities are a dangerous place to live and living in the country is the best place to grow wholesome, healthy children. Maybe you were told that living in the country is for simpletons and city living is where you'll find more opportunities to grow. Maybe you were led to believe that all people on welfare are sucking money from the government and that you're the one stuck paying for it. Maybe you were told that welfare is the only way some people can survive and without it, people would literally die. Maybe you were conditioned to believe that war is a just cause, and freedom is worth fighting for. Or maybe you were told that pacifism is the only way to live and fighting or violence of any kind, no matter the reason behind it, is wrong. We've been sold all kinds of thoughts over our lives. There are all kinds of rented thoughts around people and politics and religion, and most of them come from our families or the people we grew up around or spend a lot of time with. They come from the media we consume and the social interactions we often place ourselves in.

I can't tell you which thoughts are rented and which ones you actually own, but I can tell you that there is great value in stopping to consider it. Ask yourself if a statement rings true, if it comes from inside of you, or from inside of the mind of someone else. And if you discover it is a rented thought, ask yourself if it is one worth owning or if you might want to own a different one instead.

MUCH LIKE DISCOVERING OUR OWN SET OF VALUES, OWNING OUR THOUGHTS GIVES US A STAKE IN THIS WORLD.

Owning our own thoughts and beliefs carries substance and it matters. Owning them instead of renting from someone else serves ourselves, our communities, and the entire world.

When we find we have a different thought from the one you've been renting for a while, we ask ourselves if we need to totally evict the person who was responsible for planting it inside of us. Maybe we don't agree with them anymore, so they can't be our friend/family/coworker/churchmate. But most times, that's not necessary.

Guys, we have so much divide in our world not because of our *differing* thoughts, but because we think it's necessary to cut ourselves off from people who have different beliefs than the ones we now recognize as our own. The good news, the *great news* is that there's no need to evict the person. We can all own different thoughts and still be friends/family/coworkers/churchmates. Difference of thought shapes our world and gives it color and texture. It's easier (and healthier) to evict a *thought* than it is to evict a *person*. You can still be friends. You can still be family. You can still be coworkers and sit in the same row at church.

When a thought or a perceived belief comes into your head, particularly if it's a strong one or one borne of such certainty you won't even consider budging, I'd invite you to pause and to ask yourself if this is your own thought or one you've rented from someone else. The beauty of becoming aware of our thoughts and asking ourselves about our own beliefs? We have the capacity and the ability to choose.

REFLECTION: *Do I own my thoughts, or have I been renting them from someone else? Do I want to continue "living here" in these rented thoughts, or do I want to own something different? This week, when a particularly strong thought (usually based on opinion rather than fact) pops into my head, may I simply be aware of it and ask myself where it originated. If I determine it is a thought I've been renting, may I consider if it is one worth owning. And may I be confident in my new "ownership."*

DISCOVERING I CAN WALK AWAY

"I tend to pick up what people say about me and put it on my back and wear that label. I can choose to put it down, and I can choose to leave it there and walk away." – my friend Maggie

So much of life is about becoming. Becoming more authentic, more bold, more experienced, and more confident and simply becoming rich in the fullness and beauty of who we were created to be. I don't disagree with any of that: we are always becoming. But, I've discovered that an equal amount of life is about walking away. Walking away from situations and expectations and sometimes, it's as simple as walking away from being so damn mean to yourself.

I found in an old journal: *It's hard to be happy when someone is being mean to you all the time. Be nice to yourself.* My friend Maggie and I were having coffee one morning some years back, and she was talking about how the things that people say sometimes get together and have a party with the things she says to herself. What she said was so curious to me because I found it to be true, and I've thought of it countless times since. *I tend to pick up what people say about me and put that on my back and wear that label. But, I can choose to set it on the ground and walk away.*

The mean things people say about us, and the mean things we say about ourselves are so substantial, so weighty that when we are carrying them, our arms aren't available to hold things like beauty, joy, and purpose. Most of the time, the weight of other people's cruel words or unrealistic expectations or toxic behavior was never ours to carry in the first place. Put down the things people say about you. Let go of the labels you've put on yourself. Set them down, and simply walk away.

In my journal, I found the next thing we had talked about that morning over coffee:

MAYBE MUCH OF LIFE IS NOT ABOUT BECOMING,

BUT AS MUCH ABOUT UN-BECOMING.

Maybe a whole lot of life isn't about trying to create, but about trying to let go of what you always thought it would be. I don't have those words attributed to anyone in my journal so maybe Maggie said them or maybe I said them or maybe some wise person said them long ago, and maybe they're even printed somewhere on a refrigerator magnet or inspirational notebook cover. If not, they should be. Because I've discovered that life isn't just about becoming; not only about adding layers, but indeed also about peeling layers away like peeling off a drenched and sand-covered swimsuit after leaving the beach on a hot day. It's not easy to wiggle your way out, and it takes a lot of effort, maybe even some discomfort, but it feels so good when you're finally free. Discovery is about shedding layers and walking away from words and expectations and labels and hurts that no longer serve us.

REFLECTION: *May I identify the labels that have been placed onto my back, whether placed there by myself or by others. May I ask myself honestly which things ring true in my deepest core and which things I need to take off. When I've finally peeled away those false labels and layers, may I simply set them down and walk the other direction, resisting the urge to pick them up and carry them again.*

PART 2

The Learning

NOTES ON EXPECTATIONS

I was having a text conversation with a friend early one morning this summer. The days had been hot, and everyone everywhere was feeling just a little extra prickly. My friend offered, "I went from annoyance with snow pants laying around to now annoyance with swimsuits everywhere." She said, "I think it's ok to love my kids but hate their shit."

She wasn't looking for my advice or permission or for anything other than to vent a little, but I offered something I've been learning lately: Yes, it's ok to love your kids and hate their shit. And it's also ok to hold them accountable for keeping it where it's supposed to be. When I stumbled upon that word *accountability*, it led me to thinking about some teaching my wonderful coaches Pam and Jen have been doing with me lately: The difference between an expectation and an agreement.

I have long been one who is guilty of placing expectations upon people, usually myself but others as well. Expectations are something you place on a person like a hat. Imagine with me if you will, this absurd situation: *Here in my hands is a glossy black top hat. I love it or believe in it strongly or have some particular feelings about this hat. I'm taking this hat and placing this hat (these expectations) on your head, and smooshing it down over your hair and patting it gently. You are wearing the top hat now. The hat will be good for you, and you'll love it because I love it and so I therefore predict you'll love it, too. I'll just put it here and because you are a mind-reader, you'll automatically know what the hat is for. Yay! Aren't top hats great? Good luck, go with God and keep that hat on your head.* I'm giving you a smile, a wink wink, pointer finger shooting guns and a little side-of-mouth double click noise for good measure. Did you just try that side-of-mouth double clicky noise? You did. I had to make the sound audibly to figure out how to describe it here. And now I've definitely made the sound more times than necessary while writing this paragraph and I'm glad I'm in my home office and not in a coffee shop or they'd probably escort me out.

But back to this hat. To me, it seems well and fine and I know my own motivations and I know *how* I expect you to wear it, and for how long. But you don't, so chances are you're bewildered and wondering why you're wearing a freaking top hat. Chances are you're unclear on the purpose and of your expected role in wearing it.

I know that's an absurd example, but it illustrates what often can happen when we lay expectations on people. When we place expectations with little or no explanation or communication, it's like putting a top hat on someone's head that they didn't ask for and maybe didn't even know was coming their way. In my mind it was clear. In my mind I knew the terms of the unspoken contract, and I predicted the outcome.

I had predicted a fantastic outcome, by the way.

Except, since I never talked to you in detail about the expectation, the outcome I predicted is probably not going to be the one that actually comes to pass. *Wait, you took off the hat? I'm upset. Don't you know how much I loved that hat, and how unimaginably cool top hats are? Don't you know why I chose you to wear it? Don't you know how good it could be if you would just wear the blessed hat?*

No. You *didn't* know, and you *don't* know. Because I never communicated my parameters or expected outcome. We never even had a conversation about it. You never agreed to wear the damn hat.

Maybe you're thinking, "well, obviously I'd never do that with a stupid hat. I don't even like hats, and I especially think top hats are weird." But I bet you've placed an expectation on someone without either a) talking to them about it or b) having them agree to what you're asking. We've all done it, every single one of us. And it's not hard to imagine how communication and feelings get all jacked up when we have an expectation of someone and don't communicate our thoughts behind that expectation. Here's the kicker. Sometimes we can communicate an expectation and still be let down. Why?

Because an *expectation* that I have is not *an agreement* you and I have made together. Sometimes we communicate an expectation pretty clearly, but if the other party doesn't agree to uphold that expectation, it's almost a guarantee that we'll arrive at two different outcomes and there will be hard feelings.

I have one friend who says, "*uncommunicated* expectations are the breeding ground for resentment." I have another friend who simply says that the expectations themselves are *the cause of resentment.* They're both pretty smart friends.

So ok, the whole hat thing is an absurd example and I've never actually put a hat on someone's head, but I sure have done it when I've waited for my kids to unload the dishwasher and I've gotten pissed when they've walked past it for days. *Heathens! Don't they know they're supposed to be a productive member of this household and contribute to the greater good of mankind by unloading the freaking dishwasher? Is that so hard? Where, oh where have I failed as a mother?*

I've been guilty too, of placing some big things on people when I've put them into a position of leadership. I've had my own thoughts behind what they could do with the position, but I didn't communicate those thoughts. Or maybe I *communicated the expectations*, but never asked them their thoughts about what the position required or if they thought the requirements were something they could uphold.

The failure wasn't on the shoulders of the person I put into leadership that didn't fulfill their duties. The failure wasn't on my kids choosing not to unload the dishwasher. *The failure was on me.* If I don't clearly communicate what the parameters of a certain thing are, I can't expect another person to uphold it. And I can't just tell someone *what* to do. No, we need to talk about it together with clear conversation and make an agreement.

I've got this hat. I feel it is a good hat because of x, y, and especially because of z. I'd like to put it on your head. Is that ok? Do you feel like you could successfully wear this hat in this particular manner for a specified amount of time?

At that time, I'm giving you an opportunity to either

agree or disagree. Once we have a conversation about what I see might happen, and what you think would be a good use for the hat, then we can shake on it and come to an agreement. Agreements are vastly different than expectations.

EXPECTATIONS ARE ONE-SIDED.
AGREEMENTS ARE INCLUSIVE OF ALL PARTIES.

You cannot have accountability with an *expectation.* You can only have accountability once there has been an *agreement.* Once an agreement is made, you can go back to the person when things aren't going right and you can say, *"Hey, you and I had agreed that you'd wear the glossy black top hat for the duration of the hours you were at work. I saw you only wore it for five. What happened?"*

Big difference. Bringing it back to my early morning text conversation with my friend Erica, she had an expectation that her kids would pick up their swimsuits and put them away. She thought they'd know that she expected this because duh, doesn't everyone know that? But since they'd never talked about it, since the kids had never agreed to put their swimsuits away, and since we know that kids are filthy animals who will play dumb any chance they get so they don't have to do the thing you want them to do, she had no room for accountability.

My friend is talking to her kids today. She's going to

have a conversation where they can all agree on what's supposed to happen with the dang swimsuits. And if they can't come to an agreement? Well then, I'm sure you'll hear my friend Erica's famous f-bombs from wherever you are right now, and I'm fairly sure her kids won't see one more swimming pool during this prickly, hot summer.

REFLECTION: *May I understand the difference between an expectation and an agreement. May I strive to communicate with my people clearly, specifically, and to wait for them to reply so I know if I've simply placed an expectation . . . or if we've come to an agreement.*

NOTES ON HAVING MY EYES OPENED

Caveat: I almost cut this entire chapter. I'm worried I got the words wrong, or that my inexperience in speaking on this would lead to an offensive term or word. That is not my intent, and I did my best to get this one right. But, if I got it wrong, please let's have a conversation about it and know that I did the best I could, and I'm always striving to learn and grow and do better.

It was 2016, I was having an extended period of burnout. I was overscheduled and overstimulated and hadn't realized it until I was depressed and upset and wanted to turn my phone off and crawl into bed and not get out from under the covers for a very long time. You know, like ten weeks or so of nobody needing anything seemed sufficient. Unfortunately, that's not how life works. I was in a therapy appointment one day and telling my therapist how I just wanted to leave. Get up and leave everything. Go. Get out of here.

"Why can't you?" she asked.

Well, that was a ridiculous question because obviously my family and my business and my speaking engagements and my board meetings and my dog and my plants and my obligations. Duh.

"No, but why couldn't you just leave for a little while? Even a few days?" I hadn't ever considered the notion.

"But where would I go?" I asked her. She just looked at me, waiting for me to come up with my own answer. Damn it, I hate it when therapists do that. Finally, gently she said, "where would you want to go?" I considered for a few moments, but it wasn't long until the place came to me. It popped into my head and jumped out of my mouth: "Savannah, Georgia."

"Why?"

"I don't know. Because I've never been there." Oh, but I couldn't. No way. Coming from an upbringing and a decades-long adulthood of having not a cent to spare, it was a brand new and awkward feeling to be comfortable enough financially where I could consider a trip halfway across the country just because I wanted to get away. But what would people think? And how could I be so selfish to take a trip without a purpose?

"Melissa," she said, "if I could write a prescription for travel, I would do that for you. Even when you get out of this zip code, I've seen you come home a new person." I knew she was right, but the doubts seeped into each pore of my body. I spent the afternoon mulling it over.

That afternoon with Amanda's encouragement and help looking up flights and hotels, I did it. I booked a solo trip to Savannah, Georgia. I had no idea what was there, or what I'd do, or how I'd spend my time. Truthfully, I didn't care that much. I was getting out of this place with its noise and its people and it's constant and insistent demands for my time and attention.

I landed and rented a car and oh, how I remember that drive. I can't define the minute details of how the landscape was different, but it was. Spanish moss hung from trees everywhere I drove, and watery, swampy ditches flanked the road on either side.

My hotel was old and historic and in the middle of one of the squares for which Savannah is famous. The hotel had stairs up to the main entrance and I sat on the cool concrete each day and just watched people walk by. I noticed the feel of the breeze on my cheeks. I listened to a community band blow their trumpets and beat their drums and make beautiful and soulful music in the square in front of the hotel. The hotel was right next to a famous and historic restaurant. Something about George Washington and the Civil War, I can't recall the details now. What I do remember is this.

It was expensive. It was a luxury establishment and it felt above my class level and as I sat alone at a table next to a curtained, leaded glass window, I perused the menu and felt terribly guilty for the luxury in which I was about to indulge. I ordered my dinner. I stayed off my phone and looked around, taking in the history of the restaurant.

While I watched the restaurant and its patrons all around me, I noticed something, then immediately second guessed myself. No, that couldn't be right, could it? Was I seeing what I thought I was seeing? Surely not. But I kept paying attention.

The table next to me was filled with three couples who all appeared to be in their early to mid sixties. The grey-haired men wore button down shirts which paunched just slightly across their middles. Patterns on their pastel shirts yes, but not too loud: understated. High quality; clearly expensive. The women were lean, tastefully tanned from their hours on the pickleball court, I assumed, and they sported cap sleeves and jaunty skirts. Diamond tennis bracelets draped and dripped across their delicate wrists. Each had shoulder length hair, an unlikely blonde but not too blonde. Each looked the same. According to their boisterous conversation, they had just come from watching the Masters golf tournament in Augusta. The men laughed uproariously over glasses of expensive red wine, and the women spoke in tastefully demure voices as they reminisced about not only their most recent excursion, but with details about freshly-taken vacations to St. Marten and Greece as well.

Although their server was attentive and more than pleasant, they looked at her with evident disparagement. She was providing them with first class service. She was also overweight. Bouncy curls, expertly applied lipstick, and a beaming smile did nothing to clear the looks of disdain off of the couples' faces.

Each leaned away from her as she refreshed their water glasses, as if being around her was a cruelty by which they couldn't abide. The sleeves of her crisp white uniform strained slightly across her shoulders and the men whispered and shook their heads with disapproval every time she would walk away. One of the women rolled her eyes and made motions with her hands indicating that the server's size was exactly what they were talking about. I heard a "how could anyone let themselves. . ." The rest of the sentence was inaudible, but I didn't have to hear the end of it to understand what was being said. They weren't laughing or making fun of her, they were regarding her with complete disgust. Revulsion.

After a few minutes, the manager walked by. One of the men at the table flagged her down, leaned over and whispered something into her ear while pointing across the restaurant at their server. He shook his head and rolled his eyes as the manager listened intently. I saw the flash of embarrassment in her eyes, though I'm not sure who it was for, the server or the entitled jackhole talking to her. She nodded curtly but with professional reassurance, walked over to their server, and whispered something to her.

Eyes communicate so much, especially when they dim noticeably and are cast to the ground, even if the body language is trained not to react. The server's eyes grew wide, then she nodded once while pursing her lips. Soon, another server came over to the party of six, attending to their table. This one was tall and had a long blonde ponytail that drew a straight line down the middle of her back. She was slim. The conversation carried on. As if it had never happened. As if the fat girl hadn't just been replaced because they couldn't bear the inconvenience of seeing her. No way I had just seen that happen, right? It did. I saw it and knew I hadn't misread cues.

I was paying attention because I was alone. I wasn't interacting with anyone else at my table and I wasn't distracted by the conversation I most certainly would have been in, had someone else been there.

I emptied the lead crystal tumbler my cocktail was in and waited for the food to come, secretly hating the people at the table next to me. They would not ruin my meal, I was determined. But something else did.

I noticed that each time food came out from the kitchen, the plates were arranged on large trays and carried out of the kitchen, balanced on a shoulder of someone with dark skin. They would set up the tray jack, place the large tray on it, then step to the side and clasp their hands serenely behind their back, quietly and patiently waiting for someone with light skin to pick up the plates and serve them to the guests at their tables. Wait. What? It was almost as if the people with dark skin weren't allowed to touch the plates. I must be imagining it. So, I watched with intention for the rest of my meal and without fail, this was the way it worked. Those with dark skin brought out the trays but didn't touch the plates. They waited silently on the fringes of the room virtually unnoticed, staring straight ahead until the plates were removed from the tray by a white person. Only then would they step forward again and pick up the empty tray, fold up the tray jack, and wordlessly return to the kitchen.

Suddenly, I felt hyper aware of my surroundings. And I had lost my appetite. Come on. This kind of thing doesn't still happen, does it? A table busser, also with dark skin, walked past me. I wanted to somehow apologize. I wanted him to know I saw him, I respected him, I honored his ethnicity and his station and struggle, though I couldn't possibly begin to understand it. His eyes slid to the side. Another walked by and I did the same thing, trying to offer a smile. Trained not to make eye contact with the guests? It sure seemed like it. How could something so awful be in plain sight in front of everyone at this restaurant?

That's really the question, isn't it? How can we be around injustice and not see it? I wanted to scream, to rant, but everyone else at the restaurant was engaged in table conversation. Either in pairs or in groups, the restaurant patrons were wrapped up in the people sitting in front of them and the delicious and expensive meals being served and enjoyed. I realized that if I had been with someone, if I were not dining alone, I would have been in the same bubble of distraction. I hated that entire experience and felt icky for what I had just seen transpire. I felt awful for having been so near this obvious prejudice that had appeared in not one, but two forms in the short time I was dining, but also couldn't work out what I could do about any of it.

However, I also consider this an unintended gift of my solo travel because I never would have noticed what was happening in the layers beneath the fancy table linens and the Coastal Empire cuisine if I hadn't been dining alone. I do have countless positive stories about things I've noticed when traveling alone. But when I think of my time in Savannah, I confess that my time at this restaurant is the first thing that comes to mind. It was deeply disturbing to me that size and skin color could determine a person's perceived worth. It was disgusting. And it was eye opening. I am grateful I had open eyes to see the reality of what happens under our noses every day when we are distracted from noticing it. And I'm more apt now to put my phone down and to pay attention.

REFLECTION: *May I continue to be aware of the undercurrent of things happening all around me. May I always be searching for the things I miss if I'm not looking or listening closely. When I'm in line at a store this week, may I not reach for the distraction of my phone, but instead look around me and listen. This week, may I reflect upon not on my place in this world, but on others and on circumstances and struggles I couldn't know anything about. And as I reflect on others, may I never discount the depth of their lived experience or try to guess how it may have affected them. Instead, may I simply be aware of people and if appropriate, to ask them how they feel.*

NOTES ON FEAR - OR - WHAT ARE YOU SO AFRAID OF?

There is always danger for those who are afraid.
- George Bernard Shaw

I don't know about you, but that quote hits me in the center of my chest. I've let fear rule my life before. I admit that some days, I still do. I've feared being too much or not being enough. I've feared not getting invited to something and feeling left out and I've also feared getting asked to things I know I don't want to go to and then fearing I won't be able to figure out a way to gracefully say no thank you. I've feared too much noise and I've feared too much quiet. I've had fear in passing up opportunities to speak on stage, and I've feared being on stage and bombing so badly I'd never be trusted to be in front of an audience again.

When fear comes into my body, my heart pounds so hard I can hear the blood rushing behind my ears. My chest gets tight, and I find it hard to take breaths deep enough to fully inflate my lungs. Fear has made decisions for me in the past and if you're being honest, I bet it's made some of your decisions, too. When I began writing this book, I rented a cabin in Nebraska and stayed by myself for a week while I wrote. Fear made me second guess if the cabin I rented was the one I really wanted to be in. I mean, the cabin was way out there, and I kept telling myself, "There's no one else staying out here, and what if (robbers, peeping toms, bears, mountain lions, errant squirrels or overzealous grasshoppers, etc. etc.)

come to get me?" But I did the thing. I felt the fear and did it anyway. Why?

I WANTED TO PROVE THAT FEAR WASN'T GOING TO BE THE ONE MAKING THE DECISIONS IN THIS TRANSACTION.

And because this cabin would be the most undisturbed cabin in which to do the most effective writing. Were the nights long? Yes. My mind (fear) wanted to play tricks on me. I may or may not have slept with a can of bear spray and a mammoth chef's knife next to my bed. But I got through the nights and each day I was rewarded with quiet, peacefulness, and a feeling that I was the only person left in the world. When you're a writer and you're trying to accumulate a bunch of words and arrange them on a page, that's a blissful feeling to have.

I wrote in my journal once that *fear is an elegant and efficient machine designed by the enemy to turn people against one another*. Many of us fought fear of varying degrees during the COVID-19 pandemic. We invite fear into our living rooms every night as we tune into the evening news. We've seen it on the faces of people facing unknown medical prognoses and on the families of those who love them.

One of the most profound examples I've seen regarding fear and what it causes us to do to one another is in my favorite classic episode of The Twilight Zone. Yes, that

Twilight Zone. The old school, black and white, terrible-acting-and-all Twilight Zone. Stay with me here. The Episode from way back in 1960 was called "The Monsters are Due on Maple Street." In the episode, all these weird things begin happening in this small town. Car engines die, seemingly for no reason. The power goes out. And just when everyone comes out of their homes to converse with one another on the street about what might be happening, things all come back to life, intermittently and without pattern. It makes everyone uneasy. They speculate and they try to figure it out, but there seems to be no explanation. As car engines and lights in homes continue to turn on and off intermittently, the confusion among the neighborhood residents begins to grow into agitation, suspicion, and low-level chaos. Soon, each of the neighbors are accusing one another of somehow causing all these strange things to happen. The neighbors begin pointing fingers and hurling accusatory words, shoving one another and throwing punches. The low-level chaos has now stepped up to full disarray as each neighbor accuses the other of all manner of malice and nastiness. Amid the commotion, a shot is fired and one of the neighbors is killed. The act stuns everyone, and suddenly instead of arbitrarily accusing the person next to them as they had been doing, they all turn on the guy with the gun and accuse him of being at the root of the strange things happening. They accuse him of killing the other neighbor to "shut him up." It's craziness. It's bedlam. None of it makes sense and there is no resolution.

Slowly, the camera pans to a wide shot away from the pandemonium, first to show the surrounding neighborhood streets which are quiet and undisturbed with their power working just fine and cars running (or not running) just as one would expect. The camera angle moves up to a tall hill overlooking the neighborhood where human-looking figures from another planet stand just outside of their spaceship, witnessing it all. The aliens, unobserved from their perch far above the neighborhood, are the ones causing the power outages and the car troubles and the chaos. They're manipulating it all; manipulating everything except the people themselves, of course. The neighbors are the ones doing the harm to themselves and to one another. As they watch the neighborhood in a frenzy below, one alien says to the other, *"Humans pick the most dangerous enemy they can find, and it's themselves. All we need to do is sit back and watch."* With their mission accomplished, they board their spaceship and head to another neighborhood to cause the chaos, rinse and repeat.

Fear. The people in the previously quiet and peaceful neighborhood turned on one another because of fear.

The narration at the end of the episode is mind-blowing. In his deep and even voice, creator Rod Serling says, *"The tools of conquest do not necessarily come with bombs and explosions and fallout. There are weapons that are simply thoughts, attitudes, and prejudices, to be found only in the minds of men. For the record, prejudices can kill, and suspicion can destroy, and the thoughtless, frightened search for a scapegoat has a fallout all of its own; for the children and the children yet unborn. And the pity of it is that these things cannot be confined . . . to the Twilight Zone."*

Guys. This episode was written and aired in 1960. Over sixty years ago. We think that today's world is falling apart and that we are divided in ways we've never been divided before, but it's been happening for decades, centuries even. Fear has done that. It's unnecessary for an external enemy to destroy us when we are hell-bent on letting the fear that lives inside cause destruction. Indeed, fear is an elegant and efficient machine designed by the enemy to turn people against one another.

Fear itself tells lies. Fear steals so much from us. When I give in to it, fear leaves me anxious about even the best of moments because I'm consumed by the expectation that soon the moment will no longer be amazing and it's inevitably going to change. If I'm not careful, fear of the future robs me of the beauty of right now.

I'm a quote collector and I love the quote that says, "feel the fear and do it anyway." I'm trying more and more to live like that. It's not easy because old habits die hard and sometimes, I'm a really slow learner. In fact, right this moment the fear in my head is telling me that all these words are just a steaming pile of garbage anyway so there's really no point in continuing. I started writing this book by revisiting pages and pages of words I wrote over fourteen years ago. And you guys, they were cringey. So, fear is telling me these words are probably cringey also and not worth wasting the ink it takes to write them. Fear wants to tell us that we've stayed stagnant and shame us for it, while at the same time telling us we should just stay that way if we know what's good for us. Fear tells us that we haven't improved despite our best efforts or our deepest work. Fear wants to convince us that life experience means nothing in the grand scheme of things. Fear keeps us immobile like a flailing bug stuck in green jello, forever reliving whatever sliver of time hurt us the most. Fear wants to tell us to stop moving forward. To quit. To surrender and go back to what's comfortable. Safe. Known.

But as I've grown older, I have begun to notice a funny thing about fear. It seems that fear wants to sabotage me when I'm right on the cusp of something great. Fear sees the far-off horizon and sees the vibrant colors of possibility and wants to keep me from that horizon because what if? What if? What if I can't handle the colors? What if the vibrance is too much? What if the horizon of possibility and the future *gasp* changes me? What if I realize I'm capable of more than the safe and known life I'm living right now?

I participated in a writing retreat in California a few years ago with authors Elizabeth Gilbert and Cheryl Strayed. As one of our activities, they had us write a letter to our fear. We thanked it for the job it was trying to do and tried to identify what fear felt like it had to keep us safe from, when we looked way down inside.

See, in some instances, fear really is just trying to keep us safe. It's the one telling us all the things that could go wrong (just in case we haven't yet compiled an exhaustive list on our own) and it gives us a detailed description of the myriad of ways things probably will go wrong. As much as we want to avoid fear or pretend it doesn't exist, fear is a nervous insurance adjuster doing what it knows how to do and what it thinks will keep us safe. Safe from what? From any number of things:

Heartache.

Personal injury.

Change.

Being mauled by bears.

Embarrassment.

Car accidents.

Robbers.

Letting our family down.

Financial ruin.

Discomfort.

Making someone mad.

Community ostracization.

Smallpox.

Certain death.

But here's what it's keeping us from:

Growth.

Happiness.

Risk that could yield reward.

Authenticity that could inspire someone else.

Success.

Realizing our full potential.

Unmitigated joy.

There is so much beauty we are missing out on when we let our lives be ruled by fear. I'm trying my best to learn to work alongside of it, to make friends with it. Or at least, to make some kind of peace with it. Because if I don't, there is so much I'm missing out on. Figuring out how to walk alongside of fear and to make friends with it, respect it, and thank it for doing its job isn't for the faint of heart. I've been trying to walk that balance beam for years. Sometimes I coexist with fear, walk the balance beam gracefully and succeed. Sometimes I wobble wildly, flail and windmill my arms, and fall flat on my face. But when that does happen, I do my best to get back up. If I stay down, particularly if I stay down for long, then fear wins and I lose.

I think the trick with fear is not to let it control you. It's easy to think of all the reasons something you want might fail. That's easy as pie. *It's far more difficult to say, "but what if it doesn't fail?" What if it doesn't? What if it succeeds beyond anything I could imagine? What if, indeed?*

REFLECTION: *May I make friends with my fear and understand that it is only trying to keep me safe. May I thank fear for doing its job, but not let it rule my decisions or determine my outcomes. May I not let fear keep me down when I fall. And when I am marching bravely towards something that is significant, meaningful, and true, may I feel the fear in my heart, give it a nod, and keep marching forward.*

NOTES ON RETREAT

I am in the wild. I'm listening to birds waking one another up with their morning song. Some sing sweet, trilling, and repetitive songs while others sound louder and more insistent, squawking to announce their hierarchy to anyone who will listen. The morning feels fresh, the air at once crisp against my cheeks and yet heavy, substantial, and weighty with the moisture of morning air. I hear the crack of tree branches and falling bark as I step through the path I am making for myself. I see two fat brown squirrels chasing each other up and down the trunk of a tree, a crazy dance of hide-and-seek playing out on the path in front of me. The breeze in the blue and cloudless sky above me caresses the wings of a hawk, who lazily circles overhead on the different currents of air. I am surrounded by nature, and I am immersed in it. Not apart from it, but a piece of it. Wildlife is around me, and wildlife teems within me. Leaves crunch and disintegrate beneath my hiking boots, long fallen from the old trees in the forest around me. This is the heart of nature.

Except let's be real. My fancy Cavalier King Charles Spaniel Simon also trots happily on his leash in front of me. His tongue is lolling out the side of his mouth as he literally grins a stupid grin of happiness at this early morning walk. In a few minutes, I will take him back to the furnished, less-than-a-decade-old cabin we are currently inhabiting, and I'll wipe his paws off on the rug just inside the door, so he doesn't track mud or disintegrated leaves into our temporary abode. He will lay down on his soft dog bed (which I packed into the trunk of my car and brought along for his comfort) while I pour a fresh cup of coffee from the black Mr. Coffee maker on the kitchen counter. It will be my sixth cup of the day so far. Don't judge, we woke up at 5 am. I'll grab my 32 oz. Hazelnut Coffee Mate from the fridge and sit down on the couch next to the fireplace. I might ask Alexa to play some music for writing and she will gladly oblige because the Wi-Fi is great here and the cabin is warm and cozy and has everything I could need and almost everything I could ever want. I am in the wild, but I am in the wild on my own farm-girl-long-ago-turned-city-girl terms. You should have seen how much crap I packed into my car. I mean, it was pretty ridiculous, you guys. I stuffed half my house into that car so I could have everything I wanted here in this cabin while I am on my solo writing retreat. Candles for ambiance? Got 'em. Fresh mushrooms and garlic and Italian parsley for the spaghetti sauce I'll make later today? They're in there. Epsom salts for the baths I take every evening? Lavender, shea coconut, and hibiscus flower. Three varieties. The amount of comfort items I brought on this retreat is a little obnoxious. Ok, a lot obnoxious. But it's my retreat, so I'm doing it my way.

I delight in retreats. I've taken many retreats over the years, and they have all looked different. The first one I ever did was at a Catholic retreat center in rural South Dakota. It was lovely in its own way, but it was my first, and I remember wanting so desperately to try and "do it right," and since I'm not Catholic, I had no idea what I was doing. I came downstairs the first morning for morning prayers, prepared to petition God in my own quiet space only to find out they were something you read out of a book in a specified order, and I didn't know what page I was supposed to be on or when it was the Priest's turn to speak or my turn to respond. I mostly moved my lips when other people were reading, so it looked like I fit in just fine. Chances are I was convincing exactly no one that I had a clue what I was doing. I loved the idea of silence, and it was a mostly silent retreat, but during meal times it was acceptable and even encouraged to break the silence and chat with those around us. When we did, I felt like I was being interrogated by the others at my round table of eight. I worried they could hear my fear as I chewed and swallowed slowly, trying not to be inconspicuous. Didn't work – the spotlight was on me.

"What parish do you belong to?" someone asked, her lips pursed in expectation of my answer.

"Umm, I actually don't?" I stammered. "I'm actually not like, umm, Catholic? You know, I'm not a part of the Catholic church?" Why I felt the need to answer every question with something that sounded like another question, I'm not sure. Maybe I was searching for the right answer but doubted I'd be able to find it. Mealtimes became a sixty-minute scheduled time period of nerves and awkwardness for me, because I felt like a loud, flashing pink neon sign in a field of softly swaying lavender. Everyone just belonged there, they knew what they were doing, but I sure didn't feel like I did. Still, I found immense value in the practice of silence during everything but those mealtimes, and I wrote and walked and had silent conversations with God during my time there.

I FOUND SUCH INNER GRACE IN SITTING WITH THE DISCOMFORT OF BEING OUT OF THE BOUNDARIES OF MY COMFORT ZONE.

And when I came home, back to the real world? I had far fewer words and it felt like the volume on everyone and everything was up about three notches past what was necessary. The outside world felt so very noisy, but I came back into it with my insides far more peaceful.

A few years later I happened upon the knowledge that there was a retreat center in Cambridge, Minnesota: place called the ARC Retreat Center. It was built in 1974 and the log cabin design with has sparely furnished rooms offer only a desk, a lamp, and quilt-draped twin size bed. It feels frozen in time. Deer saunter past the windows in the early morning. Unfortunately depending upon the season, Minnesota's bird-sized mosquitos also do their best to make little vampire friends with you. The beauty of the landscape around you is indescribable in the fall. The retreat is not a silent retreat, but it is intentionally quiet. Here, you are urged to be present in the peaceful surroundings and to forego our culture's typical shallow conversation and the relative pointlessness of getting to know people that you won't likely see ever again. I visited ARC for the first time in my early to mid-thirties and though I'm typically social and love to engage with people and hear their stories, I found that keeping to myself was something I enjoyed. I didn't wear a speck of makeup or even mess with my hair for days, and nothing before or since has felt so glorious. *No one knew me, and I knew no one.* I walked the trails in the woods behind the main lodge. I came across the Hermitage; a one-room residence available for rent if you are choosing to fully retreat and not see or interact with anyone during your time there. You guys, they deliver your meals in a basket and don't even make noise when they arrive, they simply follow a predetermined schedule and set it on your front stoop. It looked super cool, this fairytale-like cottage in the woods, and I began to imagine myself there on a future visit. Until I saw the outhouse a few paces away and thought of the creatures that might like to take up residence between the cottage and the outhouse, and I decided no thank you, I prefer not to have to creep outside in the middle of the night with a flashlight if I happen to drink too much water before bed.

Back to the main lodge: in its sprawling front yard, the ARC Retreat center has a labyrinth that you can walk for healing made of smooth stones sunk into the ground in a circular pattern. They have meditation times at morning and evening, and the meals are approached as a celebration of all the earth has given us. "The Monastic way," as they describe it, where you dine mindfully with one another, sending good energy towards those sitting with you and savoring the food that's been prepared with intention and love. And I don't know how, but that food tastes different. Amplified. Elevated. Each flavor is magnified, somehow. I ate a myriad of things I'd never imagine myself eating as accustomed as I am to a good ol' American diet of burgers and fries. I ate couscous and kale. Things made with ripe plums and dried dates and bitter root vegetables. It all worked together so deliciously, and I bought a cookbook so I could expand my nutritional horizons at home once the retreat had ended. Spoiler alert: Every single damn thing tasted better at the retreat, and I found I wasn't able to duplicate that magic at home.

As I grew older in years and as my discretionary income built little by little, I chose a different kind of retreat: one where I hiked the Grand Canyon with a coach who helped me believe I could do it. The physical act of hiking the steep and dusty trails tested my physical limits, particularly as the day became scorchingly hot, but the mental game was extraordinarily harder. I had to believe I could do it, and I had to believe it deep in my very marrow. I might have learned more about the boundlessness of physical and mental limitations on that expedition than on any other before or since. I'll never forget standing on the upper rim of the canyon after having just emerged, looking back down over the vast landscape I'd just traversed, thinking, "Girl, you are capable of so much more than you give yourself credit for."

A few years later, I did another retreat with the same coach, my beloved Coach Shelli, at an opulent and posh spa resort near Red Rocks in Las Vegas. This retreat was less physical, more profoundly reflective, focused on what it means to be a woman moving into middle age and beyond. This retreat included a massage at a spa. More pampering, less physical grit. More journaling, less blisters. It was different, but it was still a retreat. I wrote. I contemplated. I deliberately took time to ponder a number of things in my life and got my monkey mind to slow down and be quiet for just a little bit. There was great personal value and meaning to be found in this retreat experience.

Before we finish talking about retreat, let's talk about Northern California and Liz Gilbert and Cheryl Strayed. I participated in a writing retreat at the 1440 Multiversity in the fall of 2018 where the two of them (my favorite authors) were speaking. The Multiversity campus was luxurious and inspired, and while I was overjoyed and grateful to be there, I had that same nagging question: *did I belong?* I was pretty sure the answer was no, and that I didn't belong there at all. I felt too big, too sparkly, I felt not "natural" enough or writerly enough. I had that feeling I've long struggled with: feeling that I was both too much and not enough at the same time. I felt "on the fringes." I spent a lot of time thinking about how I would normally cope with those feelings of discontent. I'd make friends. I'd be witty enough or graceful enough that I'd make my way to the center of social circles where we could discuss writing and books and the nuances of our varied personal lives. I'd fill my time with group activities like yoga and qi gong and hikes on the trails surrounded by redwood trees. But this time, I didn't. Instead of following my typical techniques for minimizing discomfort when I'm feeling like I don't fit in, I stayed on the fringes. I watched from afar. In the time I was spending with myself, I wrote these words:

Do it. Go on the retreat. Learn the thing you want to learn.

When you think you could go with a friend: don't.

You'll think it could be a bonding time for the both of you; it will be.

Don't bring her. Bond with yourself.

Go alone and feel loneliness. Feel unconnected. Connect with yourself.

Have conversations with strangers and talk to the stranger living inside of you.

Look into people's eyes and into your own sacred heart.

When your mind tells you it will cost too much, remind it that life has cost enough of your soul already and there's no price tag to be placed on the beauty you bring to the world when you are most wholly, fully alive.

Pursue the learning with curiosity and the loving with passion.

Go. Learn.

Meet yourself in the center of what you find.

And now here I am, almost full circle, in a cabin by myself in the middle of nowhere. I was originally booked in a different cabin but it was close to the park's visitor center and has a playground right across the road; not the idea of quiet I was seeking on this retreat. So, I swallowed my fears about being alone in the woods and switched my reservation to a cabin that's furthest from anyone. It was a good choice.

I've long loved the act of retreating. There is an unmatched bliss in breaking away from social norms, from constant communication, and from expectations over everything including the structure of your day. Here, I have no boundaries on how I choose to spend my time. I did come into this retreat with the intention of writing and that I am, but I'm also reading books and going for long walks with my dog and preparing my own meals with intention and love and eating mindfully and sending gratitude and love towards the person who prepared the meal: me. I'm eating what I want, when I want to, not because the clock says it's supper time. I'm making personal meal decisions out of hunger (and sometimes out of boredom) or because I'm choosing to take a break from writing. The point is, I'm making those decisions for me and not for anyone else or because of anyone else. How often do we do that? If you're like me, probably not that often. Retreat is an act of love towards yourself.

Here, I am breathing. Here, I am listening. Here, I am alone with my thoughts. That is uncomfortable sometimes, but growth comes from sitting with discomfort, getting curious about where it's coming from, and listening closely to what it has to say. I am intentionally disconnecting from the norms of my everyday life.

When I do retreat, I come back with a freshness that's unmatched. The colors are more vibrant. The sounds

I hear are more pronounced and I can separate them out and prioritize them instead of hearing only layered urgency and so much jumbled noise. I am a better person when I am actively in retreat, and I am a better person when I come home. I learn about myself while retreating, and I bring that learning home and into my relationships and friendships. If I'm lucky, the learning sticks. I'll be honest and tell you though, sometimes it doesn't.

Sometimes I've come home to a shitstorm and there wasn't time to continue to absorb or reflect upon what I learned. (My retreat at the posh Vegas resort happened in early March 2020, just eight days before the world shut down with a global pandemic, for example.) But still, I know I've been better for having taken the time to steal away. If you've never retreated before, I can't encourage it highly enough. Go out on a limb. You might surprise yourself by what you learn when the world's noise is removed.

If you can't retreat for hours or days, I encourage you to find moments. Moments of retreat where you can put away your phone and turn off the TV or the music and just listen to what God has to say. Maybe you retreat in a bathtub after the kids go to bed. Maybe you take a walk through your neighborhood without the family and without any music or audiobook. Heck, a retreat can even be journaling on your back porch with coffee before everyone wakes up for the day. Treat the moments like an act of retreat, and they will tell you what you need to know. It's not easy to find those moments but they are important in cultivating your best you, and I promise they are meaningful even if the time is short.

In the words of Roman emperor Marcus Aurelius, (121-180 ad) "Nowhere can a man find a quieter or more untroubled retreat than in his own soul." As much as I talk about getting away from it all to retreat, you *do* already possess all you need inside of you. Retreat physically when you are able. Retreat mentally when your soul needs it. Odds are, you need it more often than you think you do.

What could a few appropriated moments of silence do for you? If you can't get away for a week or a weekend or even for a day, take a road trip that lasts an hour. No time in your schedule whatsoever? What if you simply spent a few moments each day closing your eyes and listening to your heart? Start small. Build up. You'll be better for it.

REFLECTION: *This week, may I reflect on the moments I've been gifted with the opportunity to retreat and to recall the things I learned about myself. May I acknowledge that retreat is not a luxury, but a necessity. May I understand that I am a better person for having taken the time away. May I remember that "retreat" isn't always a physical trip away but as simple as a few moments where I've intentionally gifted myself the space of quiet peace.*

"I'm restless. Things are pulling me away.

My hair is being pulled by the stars again."

ANAIS NIN

NOTES ON RUNNING AWAY

"How did you do it? How did you finally do the thing you knew you were supposed to do with your life?" she asked me. I thought about it for a moment.

"I guess I just got tired of running away."

Make no mistake: there's a vast and perilous canyon of difference between taking a retreat for yourself and running away from yourself. Retreat connects you with the voice of your deepest truth. Retreat is an act of self-love. Running away distracts you. Running away is a trauma response that prevents you from listening to the important things your truest voice is trying to say.

When I think of running away, my first thought looks like packing bags and putting miles of distance underneath a grey ribbon of road. What we initially think of as "running away" usually looks like space and time. I've come to learn that running away isn't always about covering physical ground to get away. Guys, I'm so talented that I can run away without ever leaving my house or work. I can run away without ever leaving my chair or my cozy spot on the couch. Odds are, I'm not unique. Odds are you're just as skilled at running away as I am.

Author Steven Pressfield has a great book called the War of Art. In the book he talks about "The Resistance." No, the Resistance he's talking about isn't a group of rebel soldiers bravely fighting against evils of the Imperial Empire. (Star Wars fans? Anyone? Anyone?) Running away is a different kind of resistance. This kind of resistance is anything that keeps you from doing what you know you are meant to do. What you're called to do. Your life's work. I don't know what that is for you, but for me, my life's calling is writing. I've known since I was a young child that I wanted to be a writer when I grew up. An author. And though I have written and published one book, I have dozens more inside of me; a whole world of words just waiting to be spilled forth onto paper. And as of this writing, time is knocking on the door of ten years since I've written and published my first book. So, if I know I've got dozens of books inside of me, and I know that writing them is the call upon my life, then why wouldn't I just sit down and write them?

Because I'm skilled at running away. I'm good at giving distraction the upper hand and giving my precious minutes and hours to things that don't matter in the pursuit of my calling. Like what? Right now, I'm in a cabin in the middle of nowhere for nearly a week, a cabin booked for the sole purpose of writing. And even here, I've looked around and decided that the floor needs to be swept (like, right now) and the dishes are still on the counter from the supper I made last night and now that I've washed them, I really should put them away properly.

And since I know the maintenance guy is coming to fix the door I accidentally broke last night (that's a story for a different time) I should probably put on at least a little bit of makeup and do my hair as much as I can at a cabin where there's no hair dryer or straightening iron or hairspray. Then I should clean up the bathroom and pick up my dirty clothes off the floor because what if he sees my underwear or socks? While I'm tidying up the cabin, I should probably take out the recycling so the maintenance guy doesn't think I'm living in this cabin like a total heathen and scattering Diet Coke and White Claw cans everywhere. And all this cleaning has turned me into Pooh bear and put a rumbly in my tummy. It has made me want a tiny little snack. Hmmmm. Sweet or salty? Healthy or indulgent? Diet Coke or another cup of coffee? And after my snack, do I want to work out right away or plan some time for it a little later? Wait, did a response come in regarding the email I sent last night? No, I'm not really supposed to be checking email right now, but the reply will determine how many tickets I need to buy to this event that's coming up, and when is the ticket deadline, anyway? And while I've got my phone out, maybe I could just glance at Facebook for a few minutes and catch up on the minutiae of everyone else's lives. You know, just for a few minutes.

You see where this is going? You see what I'm doing? A few short minutes always turns into too many minutes. A quick tidying up turns into a "give a mouse a cookie" type of cleaning scenario. At home I can start a load of laundry and then fold the one that's just finished and put some clothes away and start the process all over again. But even here I'm finding my way into procrastination.

Running away isn't about miles, it's about distraction. It's maddening, and it's never ending. Here I've been gifted the opportunity to focus solely on my writing, and even in this cabin the middle of nowhere, I'm doing my best to run away. But why do we find any opportunity to avoid doing the thing we know we are supposed to do?

It's a manifestation of the fear we talked about earlier, for one thing. We. Are. Terrified of pursuing our own calling, particularly when it's one that people might not understand or support like writing or painting or music. When our calling is open to criticism or even comment, it's scary enough to run away and keep running. What if it's stupid? And what if people tell you what they think of this work you've put your heart and soul into and whatever they have to say isn't what you want to hear? What if they don't "get it," what if it's misunderstood? What if it sucks?

Better to distract yourself and run away. And while you're running, better just keep on running.

We run away from our potential not only because we fear the critics and fear getting our feelings hurt, but we run away because we are scared that if we are as gifted at this thing as we have a hunch we might be, our world will change irrevocably. Our people will change. Our lives will become different, and different is scary as hell. As Marianne Williamson says, our greatest fear is not that we are inadequate, our greatest fear is that we are powerful beyond measure.

And so we distract. We avoid. We run. And then we fall short of our potential.

I can't tell you that choosing to stay put and just do the damn thing will be the answer to all that restlessness living inside of you, but I can tell you without a shred of doubt that running away will never allow you to reach into the fullness of who you were created to be. It will never allow you to show yourself or the world what you are capable of.

RUNNING AWAY WILL NEVER GRANT YOU PEACE.

Sometimes we aren't running away from potential, we are running away from pain. We are running away from a thing that is so scary, we can't even think about turning around and looking it square in the eyes. So, we run.

One of my friends tells me about a saying they use in AA about people who try moving to a different zip code to get away from their problems. You know the kind: "I'm going to move and just give myself a fresh start." In AA they essentially say the same problems you're running away from are at the border of every state line you cross. There should be a sign at each state line that says, "Your problems are here, too." Why? Because the problems we are running away from are usually within our own flawed and human selves. Not that we are always the cause of problems, but odds are, our reaction to the situation causing the problem is what is causing us pain. And when you run, the problem runs with you. It's your shadow, and no matter how hard you try, you can't outrun it. So, then what? You can't just switch things up or change jobs or move to a different state or get new friends to get away from it? Guess you're doomed. Just kidding.

When you find yourself running, especially if you've been running for a while, I'm going to ask you to do the most radical thing: take a deep breath and stop. Stop, and then turn around. Face that shit. Figure out what you're running from, and what that running is trying to tell you. I know how scary that sounds. From experience, I know how scary that can be, how scary it is. But you'll never be able to stop running unless you figure out what exactly you're running from. Get curious about why you're avoiding the thing you know you must do. I could supply any number of, "maybe it's this or maybe it's that" guesses but choosing to stop running is a decision you have to make on your own, I can't make it for you or even with you. Discovering why you run is a quest you must embark upon alone, Young Padawan. It's daunting to ask yourself the questions that make you confront your habits, and I can guarantee it will be uncomfortable, maybe even painful. But it can also be unimaginably rewarding. If you let curiosity lead and you ask the hard questions, the progress you'll make towards self-discovery will shock and amaze you.

Ask yourself what it is that you're afraid of. And when you figure it out, put an arm around it and make friends with it. Learn about it and ask it questions from a place of curiosity, not from a place of judgement. The restlessness that makes you run might not go away entirely, but see if it gets at least a little quieter once you've made an effort to understand it. See if it finally lets you get to work on the deep and meaningful work you were put on this earth to do.

REFLECTION: *Running away doesn't always look like miles or distance. This week, help me be aware of times when I'm falling into distraction and running away. When I realize I am running, may I stop and ask why. Why am I giving in to resistance and running away? What about this is hard right now? What truth am I close to discovering? And how can I stay present, where I know I'm supposed to be? Finally, may I be courageous enough to ask what price I will pay if I don't. I'm praying you begin to recognize patterns and pitfalls, that you ask the hard questions, and that you stand firm in your space to learn the answers instead of running away.*

NOTES ON TRUSTING YOUR INNER VOICE

This chapter is all about listening. And though it seems like a chapter about trusting your inner voice should go into ***Knowing*** or even ***Growing,*** I'm keeping it here in the section called Learning because trusting myself is something I'm not even close to mastering yet. I'm still on the path right beside you. I can't say I've got this down and give you any sort of a solution, so I'm just going to walk beside you and talk to you about the ways I'm growing in the area of trusting myself. And I've been avoiding this chapter. I don't want to write it. I have tried nearly every kind of running away, distracting myself, and putting this off that I can think of. As I sit in this cabin where I'm supposed to be writing, I've played stupid games on my phone to avoid these words. I've stopped to make lunch and I've gone for walks, and I've worked out (see above chapter on ***Running Away***.) I've even had probably one more cocktail than I should have while writing by myself, but I still cannot get away from this. My mind returns here, and I know I need to come back to the page. When I find myself avoiding things this fiercely, I know I'm about to uncover something that's painful and also something of deep significance.

I want to talk about trusting yourself. Trusting your inner voice.

I find myself running away from writing about this because I don't feel like I have the qualifications to talk about it. I am not an expert on this topic; I don't know what I'm doing. I'm still learning. There have been so many times in my life where my quiet inner voice nudged me, whispered to me, spoke just a little louder to try and get my attention, and then shouted at me. These were the times where my logical brain and rational mind thought they knew better than my inner voice, so I ignored it.

I'm here telling you I have often ignored my inner voice. And I'm here to tell you why it's crucial, absolutely essential that you listen to yours, and why you don't ignore it.

What is our inner voice? Glennon Doyle calls it "your knower." Some people call it your gut. Your intuition. I like to think of it as my God voice. The one that points out your path and can keep you from stepping into potholes if you'll put your damn phone away for a minute and stop scrolling Facebook long enough to look and listen.

Your inner voice sounds like a truth you know at your deepest core, even if that truth is something you do not want to know. Your inner voice is the one that tells you to do the hard thing; rarely will it tell you to do what is easy. If you're faced with a difficult decision and you're gravitating towards the option that will result in less pain, obstacle, or confrontation? Your inner voice is probably not the one making that decision.

Some people's inner voice is louder than other peoples', but we all have one if we lean in and listen closely enough. Some of us hear it but are really good at ignoring that voice when it tries to guide us. And some of us intentionally keep our world so noisy and fast-paced, that voice can't possibly be noticed above the cacophony.

When I was six years old, I ignored my inner voice when it told me I needed to go home *right now* when my friend Maggie's dad came into her bedroom where we were playing and quietly shut the door behind him. When I was ten, my inner voice whispered that it didn't feel right going into the office of the school administrator at the "Christian" school who needed to talk to me about some concerns he had about my appearance. (Yes, really.) Turns out he wanted to trace lines across my rapidly developing upper body with a pencil to show me what was wrong with my Goodwill couture, and to criticize the fact that I didn't know I needed a bra yet. The things that weren't acceptable within the halls of a Christian school were certainly acceptable in his office based on the way he looked at me while opening the gap in my shirt with the end of that pencil. I looked straight ahead. Respected authority like I had been taught. Hushed the voice inside of me because I was a good Christian girl who listened to her elders and did what they told her to do.

When I was sixteen, I told my inner voice it had it all wrong when it told me not to go on that date with the guy that made me feel a little funny in the bottom of my stomach but was also exciting and a little wild. Probably just butterflies.

So many times when I was young, I didn't trust my inner voice. And so, for a while, I think that voice stopped talking to me. I was clearly not a good listener so what was the point? I walked around most of my twenties and some of my thirties working hard at being the obedient listener and doing what I was being told. A good daughter. A good wife. A good mom. *Good.* And if my inner voice had anything to say about any of it, I was quick to shut it down. Finally that voice was all, "fine, since you don't listen, I won't say a word. I'll just sit over here in the corner, file my nails and do my thing and watch how this all plays out."

There's a problem with ignoring or mistrusting your inner voice. Your gut is still keeping track. I highly recommend the book *The Body Keeps the Score* by Bessel van der Kolk. He is an expert on this topic and can say far more than I ever could hope to about the ways our stress and anxiety and trauma play out in our bodies when we aren't listening to what our inner voice is trying to tell us.

Even when I thought my inner voice wasn't talking to me anymore and I certainly wasn't listening, it was making a tally of all the ways I was betraying myself in order to be "good" for others. And as it was over in the corner making tick-marks on the wall, noting all the truths I was trying to avoid, the distance between truth and fiction was spanned by weight gain, stress, and a desperate attempt at overachieving. Oh, for the overachieving. I had somehow convinced myself that if the evidence could show I was *doing* good things, then surely, I would *be* good. Overachieving, by the way, is really just a cute and widely accepted manner of avoiding something, and I was avoiding that voice inside.

Among many other things that were wrong in my life, my marriage was crumbling. Like little earthquakes, sometimes the marriage would crumble substantially, and large boulders would crack and rumble away. Sometimes it was no more than a small series of cracks and fissures, a tiny mistrust or a betrayal of a white lie laced into the foundation of the marriage institution. An emotional affair. A drinking habit that we both pretended wasn't there. A covering up and sweeping over our growing debts.

We pretended though. We pretended for the sake of the kids, our parents, everyone around us. I pretended for his sake, too. He was a good man. And there were so many days I insisted it was fine, just fine, everything fine and I would dig my heels in deeper into becoming a good wife. A good mother. Good.

With every passing day that I ignored the truth of what was happening, the integrity of the institution crumbled bit by bit. But we kept patching. Spackling in a haphazard fashion with couples therapy and individual therapy and by getting ourselves to church. We were assured, influenced by elders in these religious institutions, that *God can heal any marriage. Just keep looking towards Him. Nothing is too broken for God. No one is beyond fixing.*

My inner voice tried to ask me what I felt when I heard those words. But my answer was shame. I felt shame. So, I stuffed my voice down even further. Another voice pushed through, louder, one that told me that if I'd just try harder, be better, dig deeper, the marriage could be saved. And if it couldn't be saved? Then clearly that was my fault, and I wasn't trying hard *enough.*

The thing was, we were two very different people. And to try repeatedly felt laborious, back-breaking. I know that every day isn't going to be easy in a marriage. I know some people have bad months, even bad years. But this constant toiling was grueling. Was marriage really supposed to be years and years of heavy lifting, rolling a boulder up a hill, with few periods of rest or joy in between? Just a lifetime of painfully hard work?

But the kids. I always came back to how much we both loved our kids. If there was one thing we did well together, it was how we parented those incredible children. And I knew the kids would be devastated, beyond broken. I couldn't do that to them. I couldn't. So, I ignored my inner voice. I ignored my gut, the one who dared to ask such silly questions like, *is it really supposed to feel like this?* I stuffed her down with food and with a passion for anything that kept me busy. I stuffed her down by being a dutiful wife and a good mom.

For years this continued until December 28, 2012, when I told my therapist I really didn't want to be here anymore.

"Where? You don't want to be where?"

"Here. Anywhere," I said, my flat voice sounding like it had come from somewhere else. "I just don't really want to be in this world anymore." I knew I needed to leave my husband. I knew our marriage had really ended years ago and that the spackle was cracking, and the patches just weren't holding. My own patches weren't holding me together any longer. It was a deep pain that had become intolerable, too heavy to lift and I was tired. So, so tired.

But I also believed that no one would understand. I felt I would be left without a lifeline again. We had separated briefly some years earlier, and back then when I called and told my parents we were separating, my dad said, "No you're not," as if his words could prevent it from being true. And then, he hung up on me. I heard the click on the other end of the line, then didn't hear from my parents for weeks upon weeks after that conversation. During that time of complete shattering that had happened years earlier, I was all alone. I couldn't go through that again. I couldn't bear disappointing my parents, my children, our friends, the church. And I knew in my heart that this time, no one would see it coming. My husband and I had both put so much of ourselves into trying to make it work and to keep up the appearance that things were working fine, just fine. I heard Jen Hatmaker once say something like, here's a newsflash: When you keep telling people that you are completely fine, they believe you.

So here I was, in my therapist's office in 2012.

I HAD COLLECTED IN MY HEART EVERYONE I KNEW WHO WOULD BE DISAPPOINTED IN ME AND WHEN I MEASURED THEM AGAINST MY OWN EXISTENCE, THE SUM OF THEIR ESSENTIAL HAPPINESS WEIGHED MORE THAN MY OWN.

The thought of causing brokenness the people around me was a heavier burden to bear than the thought of me leaving this world. The thought that I could just go? That thought was light, easy. That thought was bearable. That thought was an airy breath of breeze blowing dandelion seeds away into nothingness. But causing pain and suffering to others by leaving my husband? I couldn't bear the weight of lifting even the thought itself.

I had no room left for tears, only a numbing sensation that began in the center of me and spread warmly over every piece of my being. Across my shoulders and down my legs and out to the ends of my fingertips. A buoyant, warm thought. Yes. It would all be ok. Everyone would be ok. I could at last be ok. My voice was disembodied, coming from somewhere far away. I kept repeating softly, "I just think I want to go now. I just don't want to be here anymore. Ok?" My question at the end wasn't sharp or angular. It wasn't an ultimatum. It was a plea for mercy. A plea for the end to what had now become decades of ignoring my inner voice.

My therapist took what I was saying seriously enough that she called a friend of mine to drive me to Behavioral Health. Suddenly I was snapped out of that numb and disembodied state. My inner voice grew a little louder and kept asking, "Are you really doing this? Are we really doing this? Is it really this bad?"

The answer was truth: it was that bad.

I was self-conscious about being at Behavioral Health. Would anyone recognize me? The gentleman in the intake room asked me all the questions on the sheet in front of him in a calm voice. It wasn't a voice filled with sympathy exactly, but a voice that said this was what he did every day and there was nothing unusual about the process. His tone didn't belie any understanding that the world as I knew it was crashing down around me. To him, it was just moving from one question to the next on an intake form.

"You don't understand," I said finally. "I'm not like the rest of the people here. I'm a speaker and a business owner and a mom. I'm not like these people."

His fingers stopped typing, they paused above the keyboard, and his eyes softened. They met mine, focused on them. "Of course you are," he said with compassion and sincerity. "You're *just* like these people here. We all are."

We all are. We all are *them*. We all are *they*.

NO ONE IS IMMUNE FROM LIFE'S PAIN, NO MATTER WHO YOU ARE, AND NO ONE IS IMMUNE FROM NEEDING TO SEEK HELP WHEN IT GETS TO BE TOO MUCH.

I spent five days and nights in the Behavioral Health hospital wandering, dreamlike, wondering when and how I had gotten far enough off track to find my way here. My kids came to visit. My husband came to visit. My parents came to visit. All looked at me with the same measure of confusion and worry. What had they missed? Where did it go wrong? I passed the time writing. No journals were allowed, so I passed the time filling standard-issue legal pads with words and tears and reflections. I filled them with the most honest things I had let myself feel for years. *I feel like I have lost my exclamation points*, I wrote over and over, the words lining the page. I spent my days writing and making art. And I slept. I slept more deeply than I had slept in months, maybe years.

I listened to my inner voice. She had been there all along, but for a while she had paused in her fruitless efforts to convince me to slow down, to listen to my heart. For a while she had stopped trying to convince me that I was just as important as my parents, as important as my children, my husband, my friends, my church community. But here in this quiet, where there was no choice but to slow down and listen quietly, I could hear my inner voice again. *And she had a lot to say.*

The night before I went into Behavioral Health was the last night my husband and I spent together in the same house, in the same bed. He knew. He knew because he was a good man who really did just want the best for everyone, even though he couldn't be the one to give me the things I needed.

The divorce shattered my family; shattered my kids. Still today it is a gaping wound and I am awash with regret of all the things I wish I could have, would have done differently.

If I'm being honest, I still carry with me desperate wishes that their dad and I could have shown them an example of a marriage forged of trust and love and fortitude, one that would stand the test of time. I have always wanted nothing more than to be a good example to my children and I feel like I failed them here. The burden of the pain I caused them during their formative teen and preteen years is an enormous millstone around my neck. I never wanted my kids to be duffel bag kids, shuffling from one parent's house to the other, never allowed to really land anywhere.

Although I am still awash with regret, I am also filled with wishes and hopes: wishes that my children never had to hurt. Hopes that they know that fear of disappointing someone should never weigh so heavily that you count others' lives more worthy than your own and that they know getting help when you need it is not only ok, but it's the very best thing you can do for yourself and for those you love. Hopes that the stigma of advocating for your mental health is fading, and we are all making progress at pursuing honesty in relationships.

Second, I hope they see that the weight of other people's expectations or potential disappointment is something they have never been asked to carry. I hope when they find themselves carrying that impossible weight, as we all inevitably do, that they'll gently set those expectations down on the ground and walk away. They've never been yours to carry, dear ones, and they are far too heavy a burden to bear. Lastly, I hope I've taught them (sometimes by warning, sometimes by example) to listen to your inner voice. To lean in and listen closely when she's whispering to you and to sit up and pay attention when she's screaming. Your intuition is your compass. Let her guide you.

Eleanor Roosevelt is one of my favorite quotresses. She says, "Do what you feel in your heart to be right, for you'll be criticized anyway." I've learned I can't live my life without disappointing people; disappointment is inevitable. But I can trust that my inner voice has my highest interests at the enduring center of her passionately beating heart.

What has your inner voice been trying to tell you? Let it speak the truths that are at the center of your being. And when your inner voice speaks to you, make it a priority to get quiet, listen, and trust it.

REFLECTION: *May I pay attention to my inner voice, and may I trust what she's trying to tell me. When the world is noisy, may I find spots of quiet and listen. When she is telling me a truth I'm not ready to hear, may I work to at least draw closer to that truth. Above all else, may I not let the expectations of others cause me to silence her, but to trust that the only person who can know what's best for me, is me.*

NOTES ON JOY - OR - WHAT BRINGS YOU DELIGHT

You remember the old church song that went:

I've got the joy, joy, joy, joy, down in my heart." (Where?)

Down in my heart. Down in my heart. (Where?)

Down in my heart!

I've got the joy, joy, joy, joy, down in my heart. (Where?)

Down in my heart to stay.

The words are uplifting and cadenced, and the song feels like bubbling laughter. The song feels like joy itself. The joy is down in my heart! I believe that tune. Mostly. I mean, it's undeniably catchy. So many of us were fed that song in Sunday school and if you've spent any time in the church as an adult you've probably heard something like, *happiness is situational and can change from day to day, but joy comes from within.* You can always choose joy. I have bought that statement and I have sold it to others, and I've felt it with the deepest conviction. Yes. Yes. True. Joy comes from within. I can choose joy. Gentle nod.

But as I reflect on this chapter and all I want to say about joy, I go back to that Sunday school song and I get tripped up on the "down in my heart to stay" part. *To stay.* Those words make it sound like we will feel joyful all the time, skip happily, and be able to produce a platter full of joy on a moment's notice, no matter what.

That has not been my experience with joy.

Let's talk about what joy feels like. Joy is sunshine in March, when the air still holds the crisp smell of winter but the afternoon tells a story about the emerging spring ahead. When the sun is warm, and you can roll the car windows down and open the sunroof wide and you can breathe deeply, filling your lungs with freshness like you haven't been able to breathe in months. Joy is playing your favorite song on the car stereo at an obscene volume and singing with abandon, matched pitch, singing ability, and responsible adult behavior be damned. Joy is that bubbling up in the center of your chest and the tingling in your fingertips when you get good news you can't wait to share with your best friend. Joy is Elmo with his full-head smile and furry red hands in the air throwing his head back and forth. Joy is watching your children grow into amazing humans of their own, realizing wistfully that they don't need you (as much) anymore, and thanking God that they are exactly who they are.

Joy is Alfonso Ribiero doing the Carlton, it is sunshine and sparkle, it is vibrant red tulips and the promise of the season ahead. Joy is a five-year-old wiping the sleep out of their eyes and running down the stairs in their footie pajamas on Christmas morning. Joy is unstifled laughter and unexpected welcome surprises.

I *do* believe that joy comes from within. I believe joy is unshakable. I also believe that, sometimes, joy is *unreachable.* As someone who has had bouts of depression so deep, I didn't think I'd ever stop crying and attacks of anxiety so debilitating I mistrusted my ability to function, there have been times where I wanted desperately to reach my joy but couldn't find it. No matter how hard I looked, I felt like I was wandering around hopelessly in the dark without a flashlight, unable to find it. I've knocked on the door inside of myself where I was sure joy lived and I've found the knock return hollow and empty, unanswered. I've cried out in frustration: *I've felt joy before, why can't I feel it now? Where did it go?* In those seasons it's hard to recall what joy ever felt like in the first place but it seems unlikely it will return.

I don't think our joy goes away, really. I don't think it goes anywhere. But sometimes the shit in life gets so big in our hearts and minds that our ability to feel or hear anything besides the heaviness is obliterated.

When tragedy strikes and a life is lost. When a decision must be made that will cause unimaginable pain no matter the outcome. When a grey rain cloud of depression settles over my head and refuses to move on, no matter how hard I try to send it on its way. When that cloud of depression decides to keep raining, sometimes camping out above me for months. When anxiety is playing a loop of doom and self-destruction in my head, paranoia telling me that all the people think I'm a fake and no one wants to hang out with me and they're all talking about me behind my back. I've found it hard to catch my breath among all of those shitstorms, and if catching my breath seems like a herculean effort, it seems preposterous, impossible beyond reason to try and reach a place of *joy*. Joy? Are you kidding me? At a time like this?

I don't know if you relate to any of this. Maybe you can access your joy on a moment's notice, and if you can I am sending you mad claps because you are outstanding. But maybe it's been hard for you to find your joy lately, too. I do know without a shadow of a doubt that it's still there. I won't tell you, *you can choose joy anytime*, because I think *choose joy* is just a flippant phrase made by proselytizing preachers and shilled by hawkers of home decor to sell wall signs and coffee mugs that clutter up your home. To be honest, I think that whole choose joy movement is bullshit. Because I can tell you there have been times I've tried to choose joy one hundred times in a day and I haven't been able to feel a damn thing. If it was as easy as just *choosing* joy, we'd all be wearing joy around our necks like bright yellow necklaces beneath thousand-watt smiles.

In those seasons where I knock on the door and joy does not answer, I tell myself all the truths I know: that happiness is situational but joy is available if I stubbornly keep putting myself in the way of it.

I can't tell you to *choose* joy, but I can tell you to keep searching for it when you feel like you can't find it anymore. Keep digging. Like a kid on the shore looking for seashells, keep believing that joy will wash in on the next wave.

I read a quote somewhere that said, *Make a list of all the things that bring you joy. Now, make a list of all the things you do each day. Adjust accordingly.* I've searched everywhere to find who said that and credit the author of that quote, but I can't seem to find out who originally said it. If you are searching and can't seem to find your joy, make a list of the things that have brought you a feeling of joy in the past. Odds are, you haven't spent enough time doing those things lately. Sometimes joy needs to be cultivated. Convinced to come out and play again. So, make a "joy" list and try to do one or two of the things on your list.

In her book *I Guess I Haven't Learned that Yet*, author Shauna Niequist says it is our job to put ourselves in the way of joy; to put ourselves in the way of delight. And I love Shauna's second piece of advice on joy: if we wait for the bright and shiny days to experience it, we miss a myriad of gifts in the ordinary. You might be putting yourself in the way of joy and still not finding it. You might feel like giving up. I've been there, friend. You might knock on that door within you one hundred times, maybe one thousand times trying to find your joy again and get frustrated when all you're rewarded with is the returning sound of hollowness inside of you. You might be knocking again and again and still feel convinced you'll never find joy again.

One thing I know for sure is that joy truly is everlasting.

It *is* always there, it's *not* always easy to reach. But I believe you'll be able to find it again. I know it can be frustrating. Let me wipe your tears and grab ahold of your hand; together we've got this. I promise that if you keep trying, one day you'll knock on the door to joy and you'll hear a whisper-soft reply:

Hi. It's joy. I'm here. I know I've been quiet, but I am still here. You want to roll the car windows down and go for a drive?

REFLECTION: *May I always remember that joy is still inside of me, even when I can't seem to find it. If I'm feeling joyful, may I pay attention to that feeling and give gratitude for it. If I'm having a hard time reaching my joy, may I remember the things that have brought me joy in the past and move towards them. And may I always remember that seasons will come and go, but eventually my joy will speak up again.*

PART 3
The Growing

NOTES ON GROWTH

I heard a pastor once say that nothing in nature is stagnant. If things are not growing, they are dying. Nothing is static. I've spent a lot of time thinking about the truth and at the center of it all; considering how it applies to me. It stuck with me and when I'm driving in my car alone and watching the trees whizz by outside my car window, it continues to be a thought to which I return again and again. Nature, you guys. She is always in a state of either actively living or slowly dying. Trees. Flowers. Snails. And since you and I are made up of energy and cells and we are living and breathing beings, we are also nature. We could all show up wearing the same name tags at the next business mixer we attend: Hello, my name is Nature.

It's like the famous line in one of the greatest movies ever made, Shawshank Redemption, where Andy Dufresne says, "I guess it comes down to a simple choice, really. Get busy living or get busy dying." Well? How about you? Which one are you spending most of your time doing? I'm not here to preach at you, all, "life is precious! It's a gift! You should squeeze every ounce of vitality out of it that you can!" Ok, I am. But I'm also going to admit that I don't always live by the same philosophy. I mean, I think I do a lot of the time, but I still spend misuse squander my share of time scrolling social media or playing stupid games on my phone. We've talked about this. You can see it's a pattern. I'm working on it and I'm growing a lot in that area, but I'm still not a sure thing.

Scrolling and playing games and binging Netflix and watching people organize their pantry on TikTok; that's not living, friends. That's not going for growth. That's numbing. That's distracting. That's running away from doing the thing you know you need to do to grow. See **NOTES ON RUNNING AWAY.**

Ok but sometimes we think we are doing what we need to do to grow, and it's still not happening. Why? Let's talk nature again. Walk with me to the garden shed.

Every year in the spring we go shopping for our outdoor flowers. As I enter into the plastic-sided garden area that's set up every spring, I breathe deeply and my soul sighs. The smell of soil and fertilizer and the vibrance of the blooms in hanging baskets and little six packs has moved me to tears. A trip to the garden shop finds me strongly considering the wisdom in taking out a second mortgage on my home, because I'm sure I need to buy every single plant in the greenhouse.

We have an agreement that my little gets to pick a flower of her very own, one she commits to growing herself each year. Make no mistake, this is *her* plant. Last spring, she picked the flower lovingly from the sea of new blooms at the greenhouse. One tiny pink bud rested atop the waxy green leaves. As she lifted the little plant close to her face to inspect it, she declared, "this is the perfect flower."

She held it in her lap carefully during the car ride home, smiling down at its beauty and potential. The look on her face was one of reverence. When we got home, she ran to the garden shed in search of the perfect pot. She emerged just a few seconds later with a little brown clay pot, not much bigger than a coffee cup and a circumference no wider than a ripe orange. I looked at it with concern.

"That might be a little small," I said. In her nine-year-old certainty, she insisted that this was the perfect pot for her flower. She held them up together to prove her point.

"See, it's the same size as my flower." Understanding that there would be no changing her mind, I relented, and she planted her perfectly little pink flower inside.

For days, weeks even, she tended to it carefully—sometimes misting the leaves with the little green spray bottle I use when taming her hair for ponytails. Sometimes she would pour water from our pink glass water pitcher in the house. Some mornings she would burst onto the porch to check on it, wrapped in her blanket and still in her jammies. It wasn't for lack of love that this little plant wouldn't thrive.

Despite all her care though, her flower didn't grow. The one pink bud, once so proud on top of the waxy leaves, seemed afraid to unfurl its tender petals. It never bloomed. As the weeks went by, the leaves began to lose their waxiness and instead started to brown at the edges. She soon lost interest in taking care of her once-loved plant because she could no longer visualize its potential. Like most other nine-year-olds would do, she moved on.

But why wouldn't her plant grow? Why wouldn't the bud have the courage to blossom? The clay pot that was keeping it small. There just wasn't enough room for the roots to grow beyond the size they already were. They couldn't stretch out, get any extra air or food. The original size was as big as it could get in the small space. And when things in nature aren't growing, they're dying. Slowly it retreated, shrinking backwards instead of growing forward. It lost hope, and it gave up.

That's how it is with us human beings, too. When we plant ourselves in an environment that's too small, we stifle ourselves and we can't grow. A small container limits our potential. When our potential is choked out, we not only stay small, but we wither. Slowly our dreams fade; we lose hope.

You guys, I can't shout it loudly enough: Be conscious of the environment in which you're planting yourself. Be mindful of the ways you're spending your time. Be careful about the people you spend your time with. These people either help you grow or they keep you small. And when we are kept small, we begin to wither even more. The people you spend your time with are everything: your soil, your fertilizer, and your container. Are they helping cultivate you into blooming into this gorgeous being you were meant to bloom into? Or are they constricting you? Worse yet, are they plucking your leaves? You guys, you'll never grow in a place like that, with people around you who want to keep you small.

You deserve to bloom. More than deserving it, you were born to bloom. Dream big—get gorgeous with letting your heart and your talent explode into this place. Plant yourself in places where you are allowed and encouraged to flourish. You have more control over your environment than you think you do.

Controlling and cultivating your own growth environment begins with carefully choosing what we feed ourselves. I'm not solely talking about the physical food we eat, although that's incredibly important as well. Plain and simply: we feel great when we feed ourselves well, and we feel icky when we don't. But I'm also talking about the information we take in, the activities we choose, and the routines we create every day.

For me, my morning routine is everything. It sets my tone and helps me control at least the beginning of my day since a lot of things are probably going to hit me later in the day that will be outside of my circle of control. If I begin my day by working out, I feel strong and accomplished. If I start my day by going for a walk and listening to an audio book I enjoy, I'll feel nourished by the air and the story. If I sit at my kitchen island and pull out my planner while I sip my morning coffee and if I give myself stars for working out and paste little encouraging notes on the day, I'll feel prepared and empowered. And if I begin my day by writing, I know I'm right where I'm supposed to be.

If I begin my day by lying in bed and checking social media, my email, or reading news headlines, I feel deflated before I even get out of bed. My mind chatters at me and I feel like I've already lost, by some degrees. I'm less effective at batting away the things that come hurling my way. I haven't tended my soil properly and I'm less prepared for growth.

I can tell you without a shadow of a doubt that the beginning of my day has a direct reflection on how the rest of it will unfold. Doing things that grow myself? It will be a good day. I'll be ready to receive and accept and be poised for more. And even if it doesn't turn out to be a good day? At least I started off on the right foot and showed the universe I'm ready to grow.

What is your morning routine like? Are you beginning by doing something that inspires you or deflates you? Pay attention to the way you feel when you do certain activities. When was the last time you scrolled social media and felt good about yourself or the world around you when you were finished? Give yourself the gift of getting out of bed and doing something that roots you immediately in creativity, activity, or nature. No, it's not going to be easy to convince yourself to hop out of bed when your covers are so cozy. Have you ever read Mel Robbins' book The 5-Second Rule? She talks about giving yourself a countdown. 5-4-3-2-1. And one 1, that's when you do the thing. You jump out of bed. You get up off the couch. You put down your phone or you open your laptop. Use the countdown if you need to, but just get out of bed and start your day with a positive morning routine. Your future self will thank you for the habits that today's self is establishing.

REFLECTION: *Am I growing? Today and in the coming days, may I take a few extra moments and notice how the activities, environments, and people make me feel. May I stay aware of the importance of a good morning routine and prioritize engaging in things that make me feel like I'm stretching. May I* *commit to seeking growth in just one area at a time and engage in things that gently push me towards blossoming into all I am made to be.*

NOTES ON TULIPS AND REDWOODS

When I'm in nature, I see God. Particularly when I'm hiking, I see evidence of a grand design and fingerprints of intention all around me, from the vastness of the wide-open cerulean blue skies dotted with cotton ball clouds to the tiniest of flowers on the side of a hill. Being in nature is worship. Connecting with it is church. Nature has taught me so many cool things about growth and determination, femininity, and grit.

Flowers are certainly seen as one of nature's more feminine features, but flowers have tenacity and resilience. Flowers are pretty badass. My favorite flower is the tulip. In addition to being some of the first blooms to peek out in the spring, in addition to being cheerful and vibrant, tulips are phototropic. "Phototropic" means that no matter where you place them, tulips will always seek the most available source of light. Place them near a window? Gradually they will turn away from you and point their little flowered faces where they can be bathed in the sunshine.

Tulips are always seeking the light. Aren't they smart?

Tulips are also one of the few flowers in nature that will continue to grow even after they have been cut from their roots. Chop them off at the ground, and their stems continue to grow longer and lankier by the day. The size of the bloom itself continues to grow even after it's placed in a vase filled with water. I think that's such a cool trick of nature, this resilience and an unshakable growth mindset.

Whether by careless words, someone's inexcusable actions, or a situation life has presented us with, we've all been cut, sometimes in deep and cruel ways. But what if, even after being hacked away from all that is familiar, we decided to keep growing?

I want to be like tulips. I want to believe that no matter where I am in life, I will always seek the light; that I will always turn towards the things and the people that bring vibrance to this world. And I'd love to think I'm resilient like the tulip. Imagine how much more we each would be capable of if we refused to give up and decided to keep growing, even after being wounded. What if we decided to grow bigger, brighter, more vibrant than even before? I want to be a tulip when I grow up.

Now let's talk about redwoods. The tallest redwoods are sometimes 300 feet tall. Some redwoods are as tall as the Statue of Liberty. In fact, 300 feet is what you'd come up with if you ran the world's longest measuring tape from goalpost to goalpost on a regulation sized football field. In fact, the tallest redwood on record is not just 300 feet tall, but when he was last measured in 2017, he was 380 feet and one inch tall. Adding in that last inch seems like me insisting that really, I'm 5'2" and a *half* despite what my driver's license says.

Though they soar in height and magnitude, the roots of

a redwood tree are shallow. They only grow down about three to six feet into the earth. And they grow best in soil that's sandy and loamy, which doesn't hug and hold things as tightly as rich, black soil. I was astounded the first time I read that. Imagine! Instead of standing tall on their own, redwood trees are interdependent on one another. Not independent. They are *inter*dependent. Instead of their roots reaching down into the earth, the roots of a redwood tree grow outwards in long networks that intertwine with the roots of their neighboring redwood trees. They become entangled with the roots of their neighbors, and sometimes the roots even fuse with one another's. Food and water pass across their intertwined root networks and they share their resources. The strength of the collective benefits each individual tree.

Redwood trees literally use those intertwined roots to hold one another up. They can't stand alone; they need one another to survive. The same is true for humans; the same is true for us all. We cannot do this life alone. You might think you're a loner, independent and just happy as a clam about it. But if there is anything the last few years have taught us, it is how very much we need one another. Loneliness was at epidemic proportions before the pandemic. A frequently cited study from 2018 by Julianne Holt-Lunstad of Brigham Young University compared the risk effects of loneliness, isolation and weak social networks to smoking 15 cigarettes a day. And another study says that among teens, loneliness nearly doubled between 2012 and 2018.

Even if you feel like an introvert who is happier being

alone, even if you don't think you need anyone, I can promise you that someone else in this world needs *you*. They need the particular brand of magic your soul carries with it everywhere it goes.

No one redwood stands alone; it's how nature designed those trees, and I believe it's how nature designed you and me to live as well. We lean on one another so that when one is feeling weak, the other one is there to lean against.

REFLECTION: *May I understand the power that is found in nature. Like the gentle tulip, may I always seek the light and do my best to continue to grow even when wounded. And like a mighty redwood tree, may I acknowledge and understand that the network by which I am surrounded allows me to stand tall and strong. As much as I want to claim independence, may I instead lean into the idea of interdependence and let others hold me up when I am feeling weak.*

NOTES ON COMPARISON

I am a comparer. I think it's how I make sense of the world; how all of us make sense of it, to some degree. It is how I gather data and make decisions. How do the potential outcomes of decision **A** compare to the potential outcomes of decision **B**? What are the benefits in this situation as compared to a different one? How does this year compare to last year? How does this batch of spaghetti compare to my last one? (I have to ask that question because I follow recipes zero percent of the time and so virtually nothing I make tastes the same as it did the last time I made it.)

I've heard it said that comparison is the thief of joy. I've also said that comparison is the language of the small. Sometimes I'm simply comparing as a means of gathering data. But sometimes I'm comparing to build up or tear down. And I'm not proud of that.

Let me tell you, there is this girl. I sometimes think this girl is a younger and thinner and cuter version of myself. She has a cute little pixie nose (my nose has never been described as anything close to pixie) and she like, floats when she walks in gorgeous heels. I'm at an age and body type where I still wear tall heels, but sometimes feel a bit like an elephant on roller skates. I bet she doesn't have tiny broken capillary veins spidering out across her ankles. (Eyeroll.) I mean, not that I do either . . . ahem.

She is effervescence when she enters a room and makes me feel like Jr. High, all awkward and wrong-sized and out of place. You guys, this girl makes me deal in comparisons. She makes me say things to myself like, "Yeah, she has a great sense of fashion and she wears all the higher-end versions of the things you like to wear. But, you know you're smarter than she is, right?" Or, "Yeah she's vibrant and funny, but you are, too. You might even be a little funnier than she is." Or, "You're better than her because of X, Y, and Z." (Meanwhile, X, Y, and Z are none of my business, because I don't really know a thing about her X, her Y, or her Z.) When I look at her and feel jealous or threatened? I start to note all the things about her that make me feel that way, and I compare myself against her. It's not flattering and I'm not proud. But I'm saying it's true.

Back in the early 90's, we used to play Super Mario Bros. The original one, you guys, not one of the thirty-seven versions they've come out with since then. The one with green pipes that took you to underground worlds, and mushrooms and stars and red bulb flowers with large teeth. I know there are lots of versions that have similar concepts, but in the original Super Mario Bros., when Mario would catch a star, he turned into Super Mario and he grew to twice his size. When he got hit with an angry brown mushroom guy, he would shrink down to half his size. I'm embarrassingly bad at video games, so you can be assured I was frequently unsuccessful in my attempts to avoid the angry mushrooms. When this would inevitably happen (early and often, as they say) and my Mario would shrink down again, we used to exclaim, "Oh no, you lost your bigness!" That's what comparison does to me. It turns me very small and very sad. When I start comparing, I am Mario when he loses his bigness. I become small. I feel far less joy when I get into a game of comparison. I cheated, then I feel icky. Shame on me. I lose my bigness.

Comparisons are not the language I want to speak. And by comparing, I'm not only trying to prove myself and "hustle for my own worth" like Brene Brown says, but I'm also pointing out flaws I perceive others to have. Icky. It's all just gross you guys, it's all just too much. It's not who I want to be.

After agonizing over all of this for a while and deciding that I just don't like to be around this girl-never have-because of the way she makes me feel, it hits me: *she does not make me feel this way.*

I do.

This younger, cuter, pixie-nosed, graceful beauty is not responsible for making me feel this way, I am. And every time our paths cross, I have a choice: let those comparisons steal my joy or wish her all the love and light that she deserves in the world. Because in my deepest heart of hearts, I really do believe that she deserves all good things and that she is worthy of receiving them all. Just like me.

She is not, in fact, a younger and prettier and better version of me. She is not me at all. She is unique; a divine and spiritual being, a child of God who is carrying her own variety of self-consciousness issues and chances are, she has times when she compares herself to others just like I do. Whether it makes her feel sad and small like it makes me feel is none of my business.

It is my business only to smile at her, to send a prayer that she is being the best "her" that she can be and not trying to be anyone else. . .and to shine sparkling light and love and peace onto her and her path.

Song of Solomon 4:7 – "You are altogether beautiful, my love; there is no flaw in you."

She is not flawed at all, and neither am I. She is altogether beautiful. And so am I.

Is comparison the thief of joy? Or is it the thief of everything? When we compare ourselves against another human being, it's an act of downplaying and discounting our own worthiness and robbing them of theirs, too. That comparison tears down the gifts and achievements of the person to whom you are comparing yourself, and it tears down your own, too. *Stop it.* Can we just stop doing that?

REFLECTION: *Speaking in comparison is speaking the language of the small. That's a language I don't want to speak. The moments we find ourselves speaking that language of comparison are the moments when we realize that we have not been our best. These humbling moments of weakness and vulnerability and discomfort are where we recognize an ugliness within our hearts we didn't realize was taking up so much space. In these moments, the best thing we can do is close our eyes for a moment, take a deep breath, and recognize the grace we have been granted. If we're in a good place, we do our best to grant the same measure of grace to ourselves as we do to others. A little taller now we stand, shoulders back, and we rise to be who we were meant to be. Fully ourselves. Compared to no one. When we stop comparing to others, we realize that what we perceive as imperfect is perfectly beautiful.*

NOTES ON BEAUTY

After talking about comparison, this seemed a fitting place to talk about the ways we try to beautify ourselves externally in order to measure up to those around us. Are we working hard at external beautification to try and match to others, or are we doing it for ourselves? Is one better than the other? I wondered and reflected on this.

Have you ever bought hope in a jar? Given your money away for the promise of youth in a bottle? I sure have. I have straightened and whitened my teeth. I have lengthened my lashes. Botoxed my wrinkles. Colored my roots but then needed to add toner to balance out the color because the blonde wasn't, you know, just the right blonde. Too brassy. Too ashy. Too much platinum. Not enough platinum. Just, I don't know, not the blonde I was looking for. Not the one I was hoping for based upon the picture of Gwen Stefani I had clutched desperately in my hands at the salon as Julie put foils on my head until I was so foiled up, I looked like I was trying to avert Martian mind control. I clutched this picture of Gwen Stefani because her platinum is perfection. Gwen, whose long hair is full and lush and impossibly shiny. Gwen, who doesn't look one day older than she did twenty years ago. How is that possible? Is she a vampire? It must be the beauty products she uses. I should investigate immediately.

Yes, I have bought hope in a jar and color in a bottle, and I have sought the low fat, no calorie sugar substitute in an attempt to avoid packing on the pounds which will most likely prompt me to meet an early demise. But, then have discovered that it's the no calorie sugar substitute which is causing the cancer which will most likely prompt me to the early demise I was trying to postpone. I can't win. Are you with me?

I color my hair and tan my skin and sit in the nail salon for the equivalent of a full day each year while someone files and buffs and applies long acrylic fingernails to my hands and even as I type these words my nails are too long and get in the way of my writing, but girl, these things sparkle and shine.

Sephora calls me a "Friend with Benefits." Ulta has given me Diamond status, and the pierced and purple-haired girls behind the counter raise their eyebrows as I'm checking out when they see the number of loyalty points I've accumulated. When a Gen Z raises their eyebrows or reacts in any type of way, you know it must be beyond impressive, because their kind doesn't react to things. Meanwhile, I try not to react to their reaction, pretending I don't understand how I've achieved such a ranking among their customers.

I wear platform and sometimes stiletto heels that make me cranky by the end of the day and destroy my feet and cause varicose veins on my ankles. If you don't know what varicose veins are yet, let's meet back here in a few years and you can tell me what you think. They're neat. I've worn body shapers so restrictively tight I couldn't take a deep breath or make polite conversation and didn't dare eat so much as a carrot for fear it would poke out of my stomach like some misplaced snowman nose decoration. I spend way too much money and waste an exorbitant amount of time and all these things to look like a blonder, tanner, taller, slimmer, overall better version of my true self.

And hear this—I buy into all of it fully. (Pardon the pun.) I buy into it with my entire heart, soul, and pocketbook. I was thinking about this the other day, so I counted and guess what? Every morning I "rise and shine" my way through no less than twenty-six beauty products (yes, really) which separate my waking up and walking out my front door. Guess my beauty sleep isn't performing to expectation. In my bathroom, Kenra is my BFF. My moisturizer awaits my attention. My eyeshadow palettes clamor for my eyelids. I recognize the unabashed absurdity of it all. Is this face which God created so imperfect that I need twenty-six individual products to help me create this "historical fiction" version of my bubbliest and most beautiful self?

The thing is—I wonder who set this all up to begin with? Who is running this racket? Who decided that blonder, tanner, taller, slimmer was better? Who got to play "image judge and jury" and declare with one rap of the stiletto-heel shaped gavel that blinding white chicklet teeth and eyelashes that brush against my cheeks like brooms sprouting from my eyelids are the most widely-accepted definitions of beauty?

If these standards hadn't been preconceived from some glossy magazine pages then surely they were borne of some subtle Facebook ad trolling quietly on the side of my page. The picture of an ideal image to attain ever lingering in my subconscious telling me I should be working harder at it, buying more of it, wearing better of it. If these ideals weren't being created by highly skilled marketing firms spending billions of dollars to reach me and you and everyone else, would we change our idea of beauty? Would we slowly come to believe that normal was, I don't know, normal? Or maybe that natural was beauty? What if this inauthentic striving for some better version of our true selves was stripped and laid bare, exposed for the lie that maybe it really is after all?

I wonder—What if we all stopped believing in this historical fiction version of perfection all at once. Hear me out. What if, like Saul on the road to Damascus and all within the same moment, the scales fell from our highly pigmented, shimmery eyes. Would we, like Adam and Eve in the garden, look around at one another, disillusioned and embarrassed at what we've become?

And what of those brave souls who have somehow ignored the seductive siren song of Sephora and gone without makeup or the trappings of this bleached and botoxed culture all the way along? Would they point and laugh at us all as we stood there mortified, waving disapproving fingers and saying, "See! We told you all along! How deluded you've been, how silly and stupid!" Would they be the one to judge us, much like we all do with one another each day?

Come on, admit you judge others each day. You compare your heels to the woman next to you in line for coffee. You're positively jelly about the high cheekbones of the girl on the evening news, or you see a commercial with your state's political leader and you wonder if she's had her lips done. And her cheeks. And definitely, her chin. Look me in my Urban Decay-lined eyes and tell me you don't do this. Ok fine. Maybe you don't do this. But admittedly, I do. (See everything written above for confirmation.)

But back to the beauties who have long believed in their own beauty, aside from makeup and all the trappings of beauty "success." If we suddenly could see ourselves as naked without all of this, would they simply go on about their daily lives as unconcerned in that moment as they have been in all the moments which have piled up along the way leading here, and continue to focus on the things in life which really matter? The things of consequence; things that are not concerned with expending large amounts of energy and time and money on appearance, but things like creating a better future and beautifying our world instead of just our selves. Would they simply walk by us all, quite unaffected, concerned more with their internal character than with *becoming* a character? I mean that's what is happening when we do the hair and the makeup and all the things, right? We are becoming a character.

What are your reflections about beauty? I'm not saying that all these makeup products and anti-aging creams and body shapers make you or me better. That's not it at all. I do fully believe that our truest beauty comes from within. Joy is the most glowing makeup palette anyone can find. It radiates. It shines. But I do sure like my outside to feel just as sparkly and shiny as my inside.

Maybe the ones who don't do the nails and the hair and the makeup and all the things have more time to spend concerned with passionately pursuing the changes they want to see in the world, and not just the changes they want to see in the mirror. I don't know. But I *do* know I'm not ready to give it up. I reflect on it. I acknowledge the absurdity of it all. And yet, I can't quit. At least not now. I mean, I've got a hair appointment this afternoon and a coupon for Ulta and I can't quite give that up just yet. My roots have grown out and do you know how long it takes to get in to see my hair person? And as far as my Ulta coupon? Those don't come around that often. Only like once every couple of weeks. And a sale is a sale, and my diamond status is waiting.

REFLECTION: *May my inner beauty shine brighter than anything I choose to do to enhance my outer beauty. May I be not only "satisfied" with my outer self but embrace her and love her fully and accept her as she is, understanding that imperfect is actually perfect after all. And if I decide to embrace every enhancement the ads in magazines and images on social media tell me to do, may I be damn sure I'm doing it for me, and not for anyone else's approval of me. This week, I'll reflect on my motivations where my beauty routine is concerned. And I'll reflect on what the phrase "true beauty" really means to me.*

NOTES ON PARENTING

I always knew I wanted to be a young mom. Married at eighteen and giving birth to my baby girl Randi just ten months later, I have loved the learning that comes alongside parenting. Emily was born three years later, and five years after that came Brandon.

I have parented well, and I have made volumes of mistakes. Good parenting or bad parenting is both and it's neither, there is no black or white, just shades of less than or more than I have always wanted to be. There are moments I wish I could change, careless words I'd reel back into nonexistence if ever I could. There are times when I let the stress from outside my home reach the ones I loved who were inside. I'd lash out and my anger would come to the surface there instead of outside the walls of our home where it should have stayed. It's not just the things I'd totally change or take back, there are also so many things I'd do just a *little differently*, a little better. I think that's probably par for the course in parenting though, isn't it? We do the best we can with the tools we have. We try. We mess up. Hopefully we learn, grow, and try to do better next time. For all the times I've tried and fallen short of who I wanted to be as a mom, I'm astonished at the caliber of individuals my children have grown up to be.

I want to say something to you, to you moms who are just *in it* right now with the diapers and the toddler tantrums, the ones living a life where time feels like a Groundhog Day-esque loop filled with preschool drop-offs and glue sticks littering the kitchen table and you're tripping over the same shoes you know you told them to pick up at least five times already today, I have been there and there's something else coming. If you're helping your kiddos navigate the awkward preteen years and the tryouts where they don't make the team, the drama of "Frenemies" and the damage that social media wreaks upon even the most resilient of souls throughout their school years, I know it can seem overwhelming and daunting and oh, so hard.

I've got a secret for you, and I hope it helps you navigate this time you're in. Lean in close, because this one is gold, and it's like the best kept secret of all time. The thing they don't tell you in *What to Expect When You're Expecting* or any other child development book, the thing they don't prepare you for . . . is the joy you feel at their *becoming.* They don't tell you about the enjoyment and admiration that will be yours one day. I don't know why, but they don't tell you how much you'll appreciate and adore your children when they are fully grown, actual adult humans and you get to hang out with them and talk about life and discuss things like Supreme Court decisions or pruning tomato plants for optimal harvest. Sometimes you get the benefit of them calling you on the phone when they're sick to ask if they should use NyQuil or just Tylenol because they know Mom has the remedies memorized and even talking to her makes everything feel a little better. You might be in the thick of it now and I know the days are oh, so long, but in my experience the payoff is worth the struggle.

And if that isn't your experience with your older children? (Or if you are a grown child and you don't get that warm fuzzy feeling with your parents.) If you've raised the children and they have left the nest and your relationship isn't what you thought it would be? If you aren't experiencing that bond of joy and admiration with your adult children, I want you to know I see you. If you've gotten them to the place where they are functioning on their own free will and they don't need you as much anymore, but you discover that you've poured yourself into parenting and you don't know who you are without that role, please know I am holding a quiet and sacred space for you, dear one. As much as I can stand on my side of the street and say, "when kids grow up, it's awesome and you'll dance with glee," I recognize that the view might look different from where you stand. I know that "parenting payoff" is not everyone's experience.

And I recognize that many people want desperately to

become parents so they can see their children grow up, but that isn't the hand that was dealt to them. If that is the perspective you're coming from, know that I can't comprehend the devastation or isolation you might feel in that place, my friend, but I can say I love you. I can sit quietly next to you and hold your hand while you tell me what your experience is like. If you like, I don't need to say a word. I can also just sit quietly next to you and share a place of silence and breath. I won't try to fill the space with words or advice, I'll just be sitting by your side, holding your hand to support you and offering a Kleenex and a cupcake. As much as you may feel loneliness, I want to promise you that you are not alone.

REFLECTION: *May I understand that, for better or worse, seasons pass. When I'm in the middle of things may I keep in mind the grand and beautiful picture of possibility that exists beyond today. And may I keep my eyes and heart open to others whose experience differs from mine and offer the best thing I have to give: my compassion and a listening ear.*

NOTES ON PARENTING PART 2: NAVIGATING THE UNEXPECTED

Very little in parenting turns out the way you think it will. Randi, Emily, and Brandon are all older, out of the house and living on their own now. But a few years ago, this little girl Lyric came into our family's life. The journey that brought her to our family is a long story for another book that is still being written, but Lyric touched our lives briefly when she was eighteen months of age, then came back to us when she was nearly three years old. She came from a world of neglect, probable abuse, and trauma. The instability that plagued her pre-birth and early foundational years fundamentally changed the way her brain was wired. She carries with her a whole alphabet of diagnoses: Fetal Alcohol Syndrome (FAS), Reactive Attachment Disorder (RAD), Post Traumatic Stress Disorder (PTSD), Disruptive Mood Dysregulation Disorder (DMDD), Dyslexia, and Attention Deficit/ Hyperactivity Disorder (ADHD.)

A few years ago, I had the opportunity to do a TEDx talk, and I knew I'd give a talk about Lyric. Initially, I thought I'd give a beautiful, sweeping, and inspirational talk about this little girl with a tragic past that brought forth multiple challenging mental diagnoses, and the family (ours) who was committed to helping her succeed and flourish in life.

DON'T WE ALL HOPE OUR LIFE EXPERIENCES CAN BE A SHINING EXAMPLE TO OTHERS OF WHAT LOVE AND BEAUTY AND SUCCESS CAN LOOK LIKE WHEN WOVEN TOGETHER INTO A PERFECTLY STITCHED TAPESTRY?

Only, that's not exactly the way things have gone, and a shining example of beauty and success weren't truths I could tell in my TEDx talk. In fact, I'm not sure we can be held up as an example of anything except a family who has tried a thousand tries and still refuses to give up.

My TEDx talk was in August of 2020. I began my talk with those redwood trees you and I talked about in a chapter above, about how they tower so incredibly tall and how their shallow roots interlock with the roots of the trees around them, helping to collectively hold all of them up. In my TEDx Talk, I likened a redwood tree to people we watch in the public eye, people who look like they have it all together. We might assume they are like a redwood tree standing strong and resolute and independently resilient. I'm here to tell you: no one has it figured out, no one can do it alone, and no one can survive without the help of the people around them. As humans, we lean on one another to stand strong.

The phrase "it takes a village" may be a cliché, but cliches are created when something proves to be profoundly true over and over again. That's what life has been like since Lyric: we have both needed a village, and have become one. Friends have become "framily" and our support system has become like literal life support. Nothing could have prepared us for what that alphabet soup of diagnoses would mean over the long term. My best friend and I unwittingly became co-parents to this child who neither of us gave birth to, but who both of us love fiercely. And neither of us could do it without the physical, mental, and emotional support of the other.

Since she's been with our family, we have stumbled across the vast and formidable landscape of the mental healthcare system. We've researched and learned to advocate for the best services possible for her dyslexia, speech delays, and her overall learning challenges. We've navigated situations we never expected and for which there is no road map. Sometimes we watch Lyric explode beyond comprehension over what began as a small thing like her routine shifting slightly, and we are powerless to stop the hurricane of chaos that ensues. Much like a hurricane, all we can do is ride out the storm, do our best to mitigate the damage, and try to keep everyone safe. During these meltdowns our family has experienced terrifying threats and acts of violence at the hands of this child we all love so much. We've had to physically intervene and even call the police when she has tried to harm herself or run away. To say *this is not what I ever expected?* Well, that might be the understatement of the century.

No one outside of our circle of close friends and family can possibly comprehend what goes on behind closed doors, but we do our best to navigate it, ride it out, and keep going. We get up and go to work the next day. We keep dentist appointments, and we show up at Chamber ribbon cuttings and we buy bananas and put gas in our cars. A little numb sometimes, yes, but we do the things. That's all you really can do when faced with crisis, you know? You don't lay down and wallow. Ok, sometimes you lay down and wallow. But you can't stay there. After a while, you get back up and you just keep going. Moving forward is the only option.

A few years ago, I was asked to be on a Women of Influence panel with the woman who would become our state's governor, a university president, and the CEO of an international web design company. We sat in plush chairs on a stage artfully arranged to look like an inviting living room with tasteful plants and perfectly placed coffee mugs on matching side tables. The auditorium was crowded, and stage lights shone in our eyes. My smile beamed out at the crowd to convey my genuine honor at being included on this panel of exceptional women, but if anyone looked too closely, they would have seen my smile didn't fully reach my eyes.

Just a couple of hours before I sat on this stage where we were beheld as examples of success, the morning had begun with one of Lyric's violent meltdowns that had her pulling my hair, then rearing back and spitting full-on in my face. The spit had gotten in my eyes, my hair, and on the front of my suit jacket. I had to pick a different jacket last minute and change just before coming. So, that morning in that crowded auditorium, I remember looking out at the crowd, my smile plastic and pretty in the stage lights, and thinking, None of you have a clue. There's really no way you could possibly imagine what my morning was like. *You think I'm composed and collected, but the truth is I'm holding onto my spirit and emotion by a single fraying thread.*

As things have gotten worse by degrees over time, and as she has gotten older (and bigger) we've made the gut-wrenching decision of inpatient treatment multiple times when we recognized we were unable to provide what she needed at home. I fear judgement over those decisions from people who could never comprehend what life is like within our home's walls.

When Lyric went into treatment the first time, a well-meaning but uninformed and unkind acquaintance said to me, "Aren't you scared she will think you abandoned her? Don't you think she will feel like you dropped her off and aren't coming back?" *Do I think that? Yes, I think of it every second of every day, thanks.* She followed it up with, "I bet you just feel helpless, and I bet you just feel like it's your fault." *No, I've studied what early childhood trauma does to the brain and I don't feel like it's my fault, but thanks for projecting your thoughts onto my situation.*

It's something I couldn't have predicted or expected and if I'm being honest, I have often questioned my parenting ability. I've had times where my faith in both God and in myself has been shaken. Through it all, I have had long periods of time where I have not been my best self. I have felt fear and helplessness and hopelessness that has left me feeling like a husk of a human. I have had anger and sadness over everything I wish it was and over everything it will likely never be. I've felt deep grief over the picture I had in my head of how things were supposed to look and feel as she grew up in our loving home. One of the greatest human tragedies is that we create a picture in our heads of how things are supposed to be and when life deviates from that picture so severely, it's hard to come to an acceptance of what simply *is*.

And yet, as I said in my TEDx talk that night, I do my best to keep hope. Hope is what keeps us moving forward. It's what keeps Amanda and I looking for the next treatment, the next med, the next program that can help Lyric heal and become her best. We still believe her story will be one of overcoming the past and creating a life of success and love. For her. For all of us.

Dr. Bruce Perry is an expert in the field of Reactive Attachment Disorder and childhood psychiatry. He says that, by conservative estimates, about 40% of American children will have a traumatizing experience by age eighteen. But their outcome, he says, is essentially determined by how the adults in their lives stand around them. Their outcome, her outcome, can still be determined by the forest of redwoods she's surrounded with. I've found that my overall ability to be resilient is largely the same: it takes a village, and we've found ourselves one hell of a village.

I don't have a tidy bow to put on this story yet, and I'm learning that bows don't come on mental health packages. The journey is one of rough starts and stops, steps backward and forward, and some days it feels like we are back at the starting line again. I can't tell you it's all good now because the story is still being written; we are still in the middle of it.

But there are humans that look to me a lot like redwoods. They keep showing up in our lives, reaching out and asking how she's doing, how we are doing, and holding strong with us when the hurricane is in full force. That's the power we all have over one another: the power to life up or let down. I've long loved this quote from Dr. Bruce Perry:

Fire can warm or consume, water can quench or drown, wind can caress or cut. And so it is with human relationships:

we can both create and destroy, nurture and terrorize, traumatize and heal each other." – Dr. Bruce Perry

Lyric is a smart girl. She's funny, she's resourceful, and she's continually collecting an endless minutiae of details about the world that others typically miss. Her gift for detail is incredible. Yes, her diagnoses are unimaginably challenging. The violence and aggression that accompany her RAD has, at times, left me utterly broken of both body and spirit. But you know what? She didn't have the same start that other kiddos did. Despite her dyslexia diagnosis, she's a curious reader who does the best she can with her decoding skills and her commitment to continue learning. She was classified as "nonverbal" by her Department of Social Services caseworker when she was three years old and she doesn't speak with the same clarity as her peers, and maybe she never will, but she's come so far. Her full story will be in another book someday, but right now we are still in the middle of it. When I think about the future too much, I get overwhelmed. In those times, I remind myself (or my village reminds me) that life really does have to be lived one day at a time, and I've got to be satisfied we are doing all we can do for today.

I talked about my Randi, Emily, and Brandon earlier. My astonishment never wavers in the fact that from the very day she was dropped off at the cupcake shop with a pack of diapers and a plastic grocery bag with a few clothes in it, they have loved her deeply, profoundly. They've seen her best and her worst, and they've hurt with her and for her just like Amanda and I have. She is their "baby sister," and that's the beginning and the end of it.

In 2016 when the decision whether to adopt was at hand, I called a family meeting to discuss it with them. Randi was away at college most of the time, but Emily and Brandon were still at home so this decision would affect them greatly. We sat down to discuss whether adoption was the right move. Lyric had been living with us for over a year at this point, but in the eyes of the state she was still a foster child, and adoption would bring permanence. I asked the kids what they thought, encouraged them to share their feelings and have some discussion around the decision. Randi stared at me blankly, trying to understand. In fact, within a few minutes, it was clear that all three kids were confused.

I don't think I get it," she said. "I don't think I get what we are talking about."

"Well, we are talking about if Lyric stays with our family forever."

"Well, I mean, of course she does," Randi said. "She's our baby sister. I don't know why this is even a discussion." My brave and bold and pragmatic Randi. Why is this even a discussion? Emily and Brandon nodded, affirming what she was saying and casting their verbal vote. Little more was said. That was just that. I am in awe of their acceptance, their inclusivity, their love for others. When Lyric is in a good emotional space, she embodies that same kind of love and empathy for others. I credit my kids with helping model that for her.

In July of this year, Emily came across a listing for a healing retreat in New Mexico for parents of RAD children. RAD doesn't just affect the child who carries the diagnosis, it affects the entire family and parents often find themselves burned out with emotional and mental exhaustion. Emily tagged me in the post and forwarded the retreat listing to me in Messenger. The simple fact that she thought of me when she read about the retreat showed me that she sees the emotional toll this has levied over the years. I felt seen. And though your children aren't supposed to assume a caretaker role long term, in that moment I felt held. The kids are all out of the house now except for Lyric. Emily has a baby of her own and another on the way. Randi will soon be a mama, too. Watching my daughter's navigate the newness of motherhood is next-level awe-inspiring.

I don't know how I hit the jackpot with all four of these kids, but I sure did.

NOTES ON PARENTING – CONCLUSION

While writing this book, I was searching through old journals and found this poem I had written when Brandon was young. At the time I was frustrated with him because he was grumbling (much like any fourteen-year-old) over household chores. I wanted his fourteen-year-old self to understand my "why," and I wrote this:

For Brandon, Who is Fourteen

It's the reason I ask you to do things
Like mow the lawn and take out the trash

Because it isn't **my** *job –*
It's everyone's.
It's the reason I tell you, "Thank you, Sir"
– And I mean it –
When you hold the door open for me at the store.
It's the reason I ask you
To pick up your room
And start some laundry on your own
Instead of just doing it for you.
It's for her –
It's for your future wife
It's for them –
Your future coworkers
It's for all of us –
The future world
Because I'm not building a boy
I'm making a man.

He's nineteen now and has the most beautiful and smart and funny girlfriend. My neighbor texted me last week and said, "I saw Brandon and his lovely girlfriend leaving your house, and he walked around the passenger side and opened the door for her. What a great young man." My heart beamed. That wasn't a one-time thing; he does that for her every time. She has said, "he literally won't let me touch a door handle." He has an admirable work ethic and a patience for people that sometimes can get buried beneath the layers of dirt and welding dust he comes home with after his long work day, but it's there. Wow; he's really grown up. I smile when I look back on those words I wrote so many years ago. The teen years might have been tough, but they were worth it.

If you're smack dab in the middle of it right now, Mama, please know that I prayed many years that he would come back to me. When he was a teen, I felt like I had lost him, somehow. He was quiet and moody, he slept all the time and smelled like a teenage boy, and I had no idea what to talk about with him. We seemed to have no common ground from which to begin a conversation. I laid awake at night and cried and prayed that someday we'd know what to talk about. I prayed that someday he'd come back to me. I mean, not physically; once they're out of the house I want my kids to fly. But spiritually, emotionally, and conversationally. And this summer when he and his girlfriend sat on the chairs on the back porch on a random Sunday afternoon and we chatted about everything and nothing, my soul whispered, "he's home." Last Friday when they came to visit and they ended up laying on the couch, grabbing a blanket, and watching a movie in my living room even though they have homes of their own, my heart whispered, "thank you, God. Thank you for this gift of time."

REFLECTION: *May I understand that a "perfect parent" does not exist, and remember we are all just doing the best we can with the tools we have been given. May I take deep breaths as often as necessary and recognize there are different seasons to parenting: different challenges and different joys. May I carefully hold back when I have the inclination to compare my experience with that of another's, understanding that no two families and no two situations are the same. May I remember and reflect that every season, for better or for worse, does indeed pass, and may I simply rest in whatever this present season is bringing to me.*

NOTES ON SUCCESS – OR – WHAT'S BEHIND THE CURTAIN?

In his Master Class on writing, author Malcolm Gladwell talks about how humans are drawn to problems; both the ones we can solve, and those we can't. In terms of the unsolvable he says, "when we can't solve a problem, all we can do is digress." So in that same vein, I'm about to digress.

The problem, the question, the conundrum is, "what does success look like? What does it feel like? How do you know when you're there?"

Though the path has been far from direct, I've made some good decisions through my life that have gotten me from "way back there" to "here," but some days it's easy to wonder where "here" even is? Isn't it supposed to feel different? Look different? Shouldn't I wake up and feel something different than what I feel each day?

My friend Sarah is an incredible human with one of those great stories of someone who left the safety net of a great job to set out on her own as a writer and professional podcaster. After much anticipation and fear, wondering if she would have enough work or be able to pay her bills, she made the daring leap into the unknown about five years ago. She jumped. She quit her job. And to her surprise she found that when she began pursuing her own calling, not only was she able to pay her bills, but had more work coming in than she can comfortably handle. Now, she's valuing her own work which causes her clients to do the same, she's self-selecting who she wants to work with, and she's successful.

But she doesn't feel successful. In fact, she doesn't feel much of anything about it at all.

"I just thought—I don't know," she told me one day over coffee. "I don't know what I was expecting, but I don't think it's this. No one's, like, standing on the sidewalk as I go by, throwing confetti or holding a parade. I'm just working hard every day, and I don't feel any different. I guess I thought I would feel something else."

The problem people rarely talk about with success is that it doesn't feel much different. You put your head down and you put your hands to work, and sometimes when you've "arrived," it just doesn't feel that dissimilar to what it feels like when you're plugging away in the pursuit of that goal. Instead of feeling enlightened and accomplished, you tend to look around and think, is this all there is? *I thought I'd feel like I knew what I was doing by now. But I still don't feel like I know what I'm doing.* As my wise mentor Shelli says, sometimes the promise of the dream is better than the fruition of the dream. Sometimes the anticipation of great things to come are more substantive than the great things once they're in your grasp. But why?

I wonder if that ever-elusive feeling of success is a set of hopes and anticipations we put upon ourselves, or if those false expectations are set up by others. We hear what success feels like and we see people driving luxury automobiles and wearing expensive handbags and we can see what it's supposed to look like. *Yeah*, *we think. I want that.* We chase that feeling and it keeps us moving towards the next big goal because we trust there's a spectacular future ahead. But what happens when you get to the success you were seeking, you arrive at where you wanted to be, you have the means to buy the handbag and the car and still, nothing inside you feels any different?

As my friend Sarah said, there's just no validation. You don't get confetti or a grand parade. There's no one holding up a sign with your name on it like an airport chauffeur. No one tells you, "There ya go. Now you've got it. You're there." You just keep figuring it out as you go.

WE AWAIT VALIDATION THAT WILL MAKE US FEEL LIKE WE ARE DOING THINGS RIGHT.

People watch us and think we are succeeding, but we still feel a little like the sad little man behind the curtain in the Wizard of Oz, pulling levers and hustling without really knowing what we're doing. Our hope that we will figure life out along the way is a false expectation of what it will feel like when we arrive, and those false expectations set us up for thinking there's a magical unicorn at the end of the path. The trouble is, as you journey along you realize there is no unicorn, and the path just goes on forever. The end of the path does not exist. What do you get for working hard, walking tall, and braving the path? More path. And sorry, no unicorn.

So, what's the point? If success isn't all it's cracked up to be, why even shoot for it?

Because even though there's no magical unicorn nor moment of arrival, you are still rewarded along the way. And those small rewards are what you hang onto with all your might. You walk and you journey, and you find flowers if you stop to pay attention to them. You see birds flying if you take a moment to look up. Butterflies, if you slow down and watch closely. As you work hard and keep going, you are rewarded with moments of beauty. You let go of the false expectations of "what it will feel like when you're successful" by celebrating the loveliness of the small moments. Instead of metaphors, think of it this way: you get vacations if you stop long enough to take them. You get to take off early for your kids' football game, if you're disciplined enough to focus on what's more important. I have found that chasing one more email leaves me feeling drained, but chasing my grandson around on Gramma Day each week leaves me feeling energized. It really is all about the little things.

The degree of joy we find on the journey to success is our own to determine. It's a symptom of being human: we bring our own person with us wherever we go.

When you're in the struggle, you're still you inside. When you're an outward success, you're still you inside.

EXTERNAL SUCCESS IS NOT THE BIRTHPLACE OF INNER JOY.

Instead, it's best to determine who the Great and Powerful Oz really is, inside his own heart. No one can determine your definition of success besides you.

Now, when I consider what success looks and feels like, I let the moments and memories of beauty that I've encountered flash before me. I think of the flowers, the birds and the butterflies that were on my literal path on a hiking vacation. I reminisce about the retreats and long weekends with my kids. And I think of the people. Always, the people I've come across on my path.

Success, for me, really is about all those little things; the celebrations and the mini moments, not the big ones. But make no mistake, deep down inside, I'm still hoping someday for a parade and a unicorn.

REFLECTION: *May I learn and remember, as many times as I need to, that success is my own thing to determine, not anyone else's. May I understand that one person's version of success might be totally different than mine, and that doesn't diminish the meaning or depth of either definition. May I celebrate the mini moments along the way, remembering that the little, beautiful, everyday rhythms of life often mean so much more than the big moments.*

NOTES ON MEMORY

I wrote this chapter about growing when I realized I'm growing ever older. I guess it kind of snuck up on me. Maybe you're beginning to feel this way a little, too.

We stitch together the tattered timeline in our lives with the frayed thread of memory. Sometimes I think I've got the stitches of memories just about where they should be, but then I find another scrap of recollection that was supposed to fold into this sequence or that one, and I'm pulling at the stitches and changing things around again. Memories are never a sturdy garment, are they? They can't be relied upon to shield completely against the bitter winds of time, but still, they're a piece of comfort which you can shrug onto your shoulders and pull the worn and frayed edges together for some measure of recognition, some degree of warmth.

As I age, I feel the frayed thread of my own mind's recollections trying desperately to keep my memories stitched securely together but as I keep turning them over in my hands from year to year, running the cloth of the past through my mind, the pieces are becoming more careworn and threadbare. The patterns of remembrance used to be so bright, richly textured and sturdy beneath my fingers and in my mind. Now there are faint wear patterns in these pieces, the color has faded, and I see light from the other side peeking through the holes in these dear pieces of reminiscence. I don't want to see them go so I hold on more tightly, causing them to wear and fade even more quickly.

When my memory fades, literally fades like color on a cloth, I feel like I'm failing those whose memories I'm tasked with keeping. Losing memory makes me feel as if I'm not worthy of having taken part in the original moment itself, not worthy of the experience if I can't be entrusted with properly caring for the recollection once the sacredness of the instant has passed. It was mine to look after, to cherish, and it feels now like I was careless with it and didn't tend to it properly. A little like I let a plant die by forgetting to water it.

Me: *Randi, remember when you were five and you used to always sing...?*

Emily: *Mom, that was me...I was the one who always used to sing that.*

Me (not remembering, but playing it cool): *Oh yeah, that's right.*

I feel frustration and disappointment from others when this happens. I've failed in the care of the memory and by degrees, I feel like I have failed them. They say time is a thief but I disagree. Time has been not a thief, but rather a hoarder. It has filled every closet and corner and aisle of my mind with information, details, so many that I cannot keep it all sorted out. I'm shuffling hopelessly, trying to sort the precious recognitions from the inconsequential gobs of information which unapologetically bombard me every day. Lyrics from a one-hit-wonder rock song in 1998? I'm your girl, throw it at me. But the significant moments and meaningful memories? Those are the things I am distressed to find slipping away.

Sometimes I run into someone I used to know, they tell me their name and there will be a vague spark of recollection or recognition, but then nothing further. Flat. No flame of memory. In times past, there was always that spark, followed by a rush of certainty and "oh silly me, of course," then usually hugs and laughter and catching up. Now it seems the dim spark is all I'm privy to. Like a lighter that's run out of fluid and refuses to burst into flame. The remainder is left for me to try and fabricate as I go along, faking my way through a conversation. I feel like I've let that person down, too, whether they're keen to my deception of failing memory or not.

Whose mind can be trusted for a reliable remembrance of the past, when so much is colored by the wide brush strokes of age and emotion and circumstance? Dear God, I hope I'm never asked to take the witness stand for any reason. I wouldn't trust my memory to remember anything of importance. I would feel the weight and guilt of interrogation begin to rattle my calm, knocking loose any modicum of composure I've built throughout my life experience. I can't imagine my unreliable recollection being counted on to recreate the past. And yet, isn't that what we do every day?

WE STITCH TOGETHER OUR MEMORIES AND CALL THEM A LIFE.

In writing this book, I've found that memory is both fallible and surprising. There are things I didn't remember until I began writing about them. There are details that became more rich and more alive once I walked back in time and revisited them. If you're mourning the loss of a specific memory or recollection of a situation, I'd encourage you to write. Chances are, you remember more than you think you do, you just need to follow the trail of breadcrumbs back to the time, place, or person you're seeking. They're still there. Go find them. Your words will lead you.

REFLECTION: *What memories of people, places, or situations can I feel are fading? Is it a specific memory I'm trying to retrieve? May I remember what a worthy investment it is when I take the time and write about memories. Someday, the ones on paper may be the only ones I've got.*

PART 4

The Knowing

NOTES ON LEAVING YOUR COMFORT ZONE

"Why is the thing that brings you joy scarier than the things that make you melancholy?" – Me. In a journal entry long ago.

There's nothing that'll help you confront yourself more than finding old journal entries. Recently I found this long and narrative journal entry from 2014: *I'm turning 40 this year. In fact, I'm turning 40 in 20-some days. What does that mean? What does it mean to me? I was listening to Oprah and Rick Warren talk about purpose, and he said that purpose isn't laid out all at once, but rather revealed like a scroll and God unrolls just a little at a time.*

I know I am purposed to write. I just finished reading The Alchemist by Paulo Coelho. The book is about a boy in search of his treasure and his Personal Legend, which his heart tells him is to be found at the base of the pyramids. It's a long journey and he watches for omens and signs as he travels and trials to get there. Along the way, he finds a beautiful woman and a lush oasis with thousands of palm trees. He thinks he might be content to stay there and settle down into this comfortable life. But the alchemist tells the boy that if he stays in the oasis, he will be happy for a while, but eventually will become discontented and will gaze longingly towards the desert, knowing he has not fulfilled his purpose. Occasionally he will see or hear an omen which will tell him he should be pursuing his Personal Legend, but he will let those omens pass him on the wind and choose not to listen. The boy will tell himself that now he has become a respected merchant with many camels and a beautiful wife, and it would be silly to go pursue his Personal Legend. And so even though his eyes would sometimes wander towards the desert, and he will wonder what would have happened if he pursued his treasure, he would know that now it is too late. And the omens will stop speaking and he will stop listening.

How long? How long until those voices to stop speaking once we stop listening?

People who know me well must wonder what I'm doing, fluttering my wings discontentedly, beating them madly against myself.

So, I second guess myself and ask: what am I supposed to write anyway? A book? A poem? A newspaper column? And because I can't precisely answer that question, I settle my winds and rest in the familiar thrum of seasons and the known oasis of Oh My Cupcakes!

What do I know for sure? That I don't know anything for sure. And that I'm probably copping out by taking that way out. I don't know what my words are supposed to be, but I do know I'm supposed to be writing them. I've learned there is so much that I don't know. I now find so much gray in this world that keeps insisting on being black and white.

This is not the book about Oh My Cupcakes that I thought God would give to me. But what if my purpose was never to write the book about how glorious our success was, but instead about how I continued to pursue other things He was calling me to do?

What if it's both?

Ouch. Those words slice through me as I read them.

Why? Because I found them in a folder of my writing from eight years ago. I had been in the middle of writing my first book about Oh My Cupcakes!, and was wrestling with what I thought people would want to read versus what I felt called to write about.

Nearly three thousand days of my life have happened since that journal entry. Over 70,000 hours have passed me by since I wrote those words and since my conviction and knowing of what I was supposed to be doing was laid bare on the pages for me and God to see.

I did write that book about Oh My Cupcakes! and in the end, *the book I thought people would want to read* won out, and that's the one I wrote. I remember the day the first printed copies of the book were delivered. I opened the cardboard box and as I reached in and ran my fingers over the soft grey and pink cover of the book, a voice inside me said, *you took the easy way out on this one, kid. You didn't have to risk much to write this book.*

A lot has happened since I wrote that book. In eight years, I've adopted a child and gone to Europe and grown children and a grandson, planted four gardens and cultivated countless wrinkles. In eight years we've weathered different seasons of management and I've seen dozens of people come and go from my business. A few of them who had once told me, *"When I start something, I'm the type of person that's in it for the long haul. You can count on me. I'm committed."* And still, as if refusing to listen to the whispering voice of my personal legend or my screaming voice of my own intuition, I have been running in the same familiar track for the last eight years. Those people have gone, and I am still here. The book I wrote about Oh My Cupcakes! wasn't the one filled with inconvenient truths about how sloppy and heartbreaking business can sometimes be. I didn't write the book that told the reality of nagging, sometimes relentless self-doubt or the one about bank accounts and banks of peaceful sleep that both become frightfully low during slow season. It wasn't the book that talked about how heart-shattering and panic-inducing it is when the people on whom you've counted change their mind and leave to pursue something different. I didn't write about that. I wrote a book about my business ventures and that book wasn't the one I felt *compelled* to write, it was the one I thought I should write. Back then, I didn't write a book about leaving my comfort zone, because I felt I couldn't. It wouldn't have been truth, because back then I was unable. It was too risky. Not only for me, but for the dozens of people whose livelihoods count on the success of the company.

People often think of risk in terms of venturing out on a limb and starting something new; untested and unknown. A startup company. A wedding proposal. A move to a new city. Heck, even a bold new hairstyle.

But we need to acknowledge the fact that starting something new means the ending of something else, and that's equally as scary. In fact, is it equally as scary, or is it even scarier? Isn't there even more risk in making a conscious choice to step away from something that is comfortable, successful, and known?

Being an entrepreneur is one thing; people celebrate that: people admire your moxie and your belief in yourself. But deliberately moving away from something stable that you have built? That's a different story entirely. That decision involves a lot of explanation and floundering about. Justifying. Answering *why* to a thousand confused people asking the question.

It's taken me eight years. It's still a work in progress, but leaving my comfort zone is happening, by degrees. I don't follow Rick Warren these days like I did eight years ago when I wrote those words about purpose. But I do think he was right when he said it doesn't happen all at once. He was right when he said that God unrolls the scroll little by little. As I look back, I understand that's exactly how it has been happening. During some years I've only gotten an inch or so of new scroll sent my way, but other years I've gotten yards and yards of it. I'm in a yards and yards year now, and I'm growing ever more confident about following my purpose. I've lost the impatience I had back then, and I'm trusting the process of how it's all playing out. God keeps putting the right people in my path to make things happen not only for me, but for them too, as I watch them grow into their own strength and gifts. They are leading. I am cheering them on.

I've realized my vision has evolved over time as well. I've gained more clarity on the direction I want to follow. My love for the company I founded is a different kind of love now. It's like the love you feel when your child goes to college and you marvel with pride at everything they already are, and everything they will surely become. It's a different kind of love than the one that gets up for 3 am feedings or drives the school carpool, but it's still love.

I've gained more clarity on the direction I want to follow and in fact, it doesn't look as much like stepping *away* from my business ventures as it is stepping *into* my purpose within the walls of Oh My Cupcakes! and outside of them. I am evolving in my strengths and honing in on the things I know I'm passionate about and really good at. I am becoming that Professional Encourager I've long wanted to be. And I'm now convinced that I haven't lost as many years as I thought. My purpose has been going through a process of growth and refinement just as I have.

"To use my skills, experiences, and talents to help people. To grow myself through my vocation as well as by seeking new opportunities for personal growth. To help grow women, ensuring them that, no matter their circumstances or their past, they are beautiful, strong, and empowered women through Christ." That was my purpose then, and it's my purpose now. But I'm gaining clarity on just how to make that purpose come to life. And though I don't know much, I know that all those things are coming together for such a risk-taking time as this.

What are the areas you feel the whisper of growth calling you, but you're afraid to even acknowledge its voice? Is it a relationship you need to pursue? A relationship you need to end? Maybe it's a calling you've had placed upon your heart, but it seems silly to think about following it.

WEIGH THE TRUE RISK OF FOLLOWING YOUR CALLING. AGAINST THAT, WEIGH THE RISK OF NOT FOLLOWING IT.

When we aren't pursuing the truest passions God has placed in our hearts, the stress we feel inside ends up coming out sideways. For me, it has looked like bouts of extreme anxiety, grey seasons of depression and malaise, and excess physical weight that just won't leave my frame no matter what changes I make to my diet or activity level. Make no mistake, there is a cost high associated with not following your calling in life, and it's more than just mental discomfort.

If you don't know exactly what that passion is just yet? Don't worry about that. You'll find it when it's the right time. As the author Elizabeth Gilbert says in her book *Big Magic: Creative Living Beyond Fear*, take a closer look at the things which make you curious. The things that make you turn your chin a quarter inch and say to yourself, "I want to know more about that." She says there's no shame, and in fact there is great reward to be found in flitting from thing to thing like a hummingbird. That's curiosity.

Following curiosity will lead you to discovery. Following discovery will lead you to the things you'll find you're deeply passionate about. Following your passions will lead you to your purpose. It's up to you to be brave enough to step out of your comfort zone and into that purpose once it has been revealed.

REFLECTION: *May I keep my ears open to the voices guiding me towards my purpose and calling in life. And when I identify what that purpose is, may I have the courage to step out of the oasis of what is comfortable and known, and step into the fullness of who I am made to be.*

I AM THE ONE WHO . . .

I was in a conversation with my friend Pamela a few months back. Pamela is a hug personified. If you looked up the word "nurture" in the dictionary, you'll see her fiery red hair, glasses, and her warmly smiling face alongside of it. She is a wonder of spiritual proportions, a pipeline of intuition. She is a woman who looks at you and just knows if your day is going well, if it's headed down a hard path, or if you're facing challenge. She just knows. And usually, she's right on, leaving you to sort of wonder if she's been inside your head or if she's secretly been following you around all day.

That sunny afternoon, Pamela and I conversed in her garden-level living room. While we talked, she looked at me intently, her eyes narrowing. Finally, she said, "ever since you got here today, I hear the same words in my head, over and over.

"What words?" I asked, curious.

"I am the one who."

"I am the one who *what?*" I asked her. She just shrugged and said she guessed it was up to me to figure out. I wondered what she meant. She started asking me a couple of questions.

"Do you feel like you've lost the power of your own voice, sometimes?" Taking cues from some things we had talked about and sprinkling in a heavy dose of intuition, she knew the answer was a resounding yes. But she didn't stop there.

"Are you on the verge of finding that voice back again?" I nodded. I had been doing a lot of personal work (yay, therapy!) which was directing me to a new place of confidence and empowerment.

I am the one who. Her questions made sense and like gears turning swiftly and locks clacking and opening, things grew clearer in my head. *I am the one who – it was up to me to complete that statement.* No one else could make the moves for me, it was up to me to decide what the next steps were and which direction I was going.

I came home and feverishly began to free-write. I jotted down every statement that popped into my head, even if it didn't seem relevant or I didn't understand quite what the words meant, I just wrote.

I am the one who began this.

I am the one who is writing this story.

I am the one in charge of my happiness.

I am the one who can make a difference.

I am the one who is in charge of my own health.

I am the one who is in charge of my own outcome.

I am the one who likes to see everyone included.

I am the one who loves bright colors.

I am the one who likes to be an encourager.

I am the one who receives joy from giving to others.

I am the one who can decide when to tap out.

I am the one who decides when I go to bed.

I am the one who is a seeker.

I am the one who is healthy and alive.

I am the one who has published a book.

I am the one who is going to decide if I write or not.

I am the one who is going to dictate how my time is spent.

I am the one who will say when this is over.

I am the one who is responsible for my own happiness.

I am the one who decides what I read.

I am the one who invested a lot of money into my businesses.

I am the one who can decide how much time I put into them.

I am the one who gets to make my own rules.

I am the one who can change the world.

I am the one who is the best mom I can be.

I am the one who tries hard but sometimes could try harder.

I am the one who loves to give generously.

I am the one who has overcome.

I am the one who is resilient.

I am the one who is tired.

I am the one who is a highly functioning introvert.

I am the one who loves people.

I am the one who will answer for how I've spent my life.

I am the one who will hold regret if I don't focus more.

I am the one who chooses who I give my energy to.

I am the one who does the best I can with what I have.

I am the one who will never stop trying.

I don't know where many of those "I am the One Who" statements originated from. But I've learned enough to know that when we allow our minds the independence of free writing, our subconscious brings things to light things with which we didn't even know we were grappling. If we allow those deeply held secrets (secrets we've been keeping even from ourselves) to come to the forefront and give them freedom and a little breathing room, we look back and find some incredible a-ha moments.

OFTEN, WHEN WE HAVE THE COURAGE TO TAKE OWNERSHIP OF OUR IDEAS, WE FIND ANSWERS TO QUESTIONS WE DIDN'T EVEN KNOW WERE INSIDE OF US.

Sometimes when we start with, "I am the one who," we find our next right steps in the completion of that phrase.

No, I didn't know where those statements came from, but I know that when I wrote them, I felt powerful. I felt like Alice in Wonderland ala the 2000's era Tim Burton movie. In a particular scene in the movie, she realizes she's getting tired of being pushed around. She's fed up, and she's coming back into her own power.

In that scene, she says, *"From the moment I fell down that rabbit hole I've been told where I must go and who I must be. I've been shrunk, stretched, scratched, and stuffed into a teapot. I've been accused of being Alice and of not being Alice but this is my dream. I'll decide where it goes from here."*

She was the one who would decide. I am the one who.

In those statements, we find our power. We discover our voice. And we realize that both have been with us, inside of us all the time. Writing and reciting, "I am the one who" has been one of the single most empowering and action-provoking exercises I've ever done.

And it can be for you, too. It's that moment or series of moments when you stop listening to what others say you should do and you start saying, *"I am the one who will determine where I'm going from here."*

I am the one who. You are the one who. No one besides you. No one is going to tell you when it's time to take the leap. No one is going to tell you which date on the calendar is the right date to do the thing. When we finally find our voice and learn that we get to name a goal, go after it, or even choose not to go after it, that's success. This might be the perfect time, or it might not be. If it's not, that's totally ok. But be sure you're listening to things like intuition and logic and truth rather than to fear. Trust the voice that tells you that you can, rather than the one that tells you the reasons you *can't*. If you write your I am the One Who statements, and you still don't know? Get quiet and listen. Our world clamors for every bit of our attention and energy. Move away from the noise and move into yourself. Deep down in the center of your being, you are the one who knows. You are the one who believes. Believe it. Whatever it is, you've got to believe in *it*, believe in *yourself*, and chase the hell after it.

REFLECTION: *May I spend time this week journaling with the statement, "I am the one who." May I listen to intuition and not to fear. And if I already know the answer to that question and the answer is yes, may I have the courage to race towards my goal with longing like a ravenous toddler sprinting towards fruit snacks.*

NOTES ON RISK

Some of the world's greatest feats were accomplished by people not smart enough to know they were impossible.

- Doug Larson

I've always been a bit of a risk-taker.

When I was in high school, I decided to ask if I could graduate early, at semester time. The school guidance counselor Mr. Jackson looked up at me dubiously. No one had graduated early in over ten years, he told me. Why? Because no one had asked.

Well, I'm asking.

And I persisted. I stopped by his office every day. Had he talked to whoever he needed to talk to yet? Had he found out whatever he needed to find out so I could graduate early? One day he sighed, rolled his eyes, and said OK. I had worn him down.

And so, I graduated at the end of the first semester, and I got out of high school early. And while my peers were going to basketball games and parties I hadn't been invited to anyway, I was working my first fulltime job. You guys, I had business cards and a four-word job title. I felt so grown up, a real professional. Then, just a few months later, I fell to the very grown up and unfortunate side of a 20% company downsizing and got laid off from my first fulltime job before my classmates had even walked the stage at graduation. I did what most any eighteen-year-old, unmarried-and-no-children young woman would do: I decided I'd open an in-home daycare. I ran a successful daycare for a few years and took care of people's babies. Ironically, I did this until I had kids of my own and didn't want to share my precious family time with other people's babies while my own babies were so little.

I had many small businesses, some that turned out to be big businesses. I had a minimally successful side hustle selling expensive scrapbooking supplies. Turns out, when you carry inventory of all the supplies and also you really want to just *do the scrapbooking* instead of *selling the scrapbooking*, your profits are chewed up pretty quickly.

I had an incredibly successful side hustle stint as a Pure Romance consultant. My tax man was impressed when he was all, "Really? You sold *how much* this year?" I think I helped make a lot of women happy. Haven't heard of Pure Romance? Google it if you're not familiar, but not in front of the kids or while you're at work. Sorry to my children; I hope I haven't shattered the innocence of your childhood when you realize what kind of parties mom was gone hosting for other moms every Friday and Saturday night.

I worked many jobs in between side hustles (or vice versa) and then in 2009, I finally made my way to opening a full-scale brick and mortar cupcake company.

I've never shied away from risk. Part of me has always believed that if I mess up, I'll just go grab an hourly wage job and scrape my way back out of it. Now that I'm a business owner who employs over forty people, the flippancy doesn't fly from that statement quite as easily as it used to. Now I'm acutely aware that over forty separate people depend upon my decision-making abilities to influence our company's success which will in turn warrant they can make their car payments and buy groceries and pay for football uniforms for their kids. It's a different kind of risk, but it's still a risk I take every day.

Risk is a funny thing. It's not that you either have it or you don't. Risk ebbs and flows.

THERE ARE TIMES I FEEL SO BRAVE AND READY TO MAKE A LEAP THAT OTHERS MUST SERVE ME A DOSE OF REALITY AND HOLD ME BACK. THERE ARE TIMES WHEN I'M WORRYING OVER NOTHING, FEEL PARALYZED, AND I FEAR SMALL DETAILS WILL RESULT IN CATASTROPHIC OUTCOMES.

Risk. Financial advisors call it risk tolerance or risk aversion. Where do you fall on the spectrum today? Whatever your tolerance for risk, good on you. If you're one who will gladly go ziplining and jump out of an airplane and give your heart to others knowing it might end up shattered, I respect you so damn much. I see you and I am here for it. You inspire me. And if you're one who's more methodical about your decision making and gathers the information before making a move, I applaud that as well. Friends, you are the ones that restrain us from making ridiculous leaps without having the necessary details. We need both personalities in this world.

We need both personalities in our friendships as well. We need the friends who will say, "Come on, let's just go for it! What's the worst that could happen?" all while you're silently cataloging the multitude of things that definitely could go wrong. My boat could get a hole in it, my parachute could fail to open, my kayak could overturn, my mini scooter could get hit by a bus in traffic. *There are a million unlikely scenarios I could dream up.*

But we also need friends who will tell us with love and truth all the reality-based scenarios that could occur, so we slow our roll a little bit when we've got a big idea and consider if scaling that 3' wide section of Angel's Landing with 2,000 foot drop-offs on either side is really that important to us or not. We need a balance of both.

Let's talk about how it feels to risk and to lose. Or to risk and get hurt. Usually, people and messy feelings are wrapped up in that, right? I've gotten hurt so many times when I have gone out on a limb for someone who wanted a job and I've given them a second chance when no one else would. I am the Queen of Believing in People, and I believe in second chances. By default, this also makes me the Queen of Getting Hurt when giving someone a second chance has on multiple occasions crashed and burned spectacularly in a fiery pile of flames and destruction.

I mean, occasionally it has ended up ok. I'm sure if I think hard, I can recall a time when I took a risk and gave someone a second chance and it turned out great. Though as I rifle back through memories and remember money being stolen, unidentifiable pills being found on the floor of the staff closet at work, my name being slandered online and beyond, and good people walking away because I was investing more time on the people I was hell-bent on saving, it's hard to remember times that risk turned out well. Can I be real with you? More often than not it's ended up disastrously. Taking risks on people has ended up with heartache by the bucketful.

On the smoke and ash of those disasters it's tempting to be like, "Screw that. I'm never doing this again. I'm never putting myself out there to get shit on like this again. It hurts too much." And when it happens, I do use that whole vernacular and mantra for a couple of days. *I'm never taking a chance on another person. Why would I put myself up for the hurt, willingly, over and over? It's stupid. I must be the stupidest person who ever lived.*

But within a few days and after downing a couple of bags of chips and salsa, it seems God always puts another perspective in my path. One where He shows me that a risk I took somewhere along the way resulted in something good. Sometimes it has come back in the form of, "My daughter worked for your company years ago, and I want you to know she says it's the best job she ever worked." Or it can come back in a random person telling me that something I said made them start believing in themselves. And then smile slightly, I roll my eyes at God and begrudgingly admit that it's worth it. But for the record? I also tell God how pissed I am at Him for making me go through the hurt and heartache. Then I eat more chips and salsa and I calm down.

When you put yourself out there, whether in a business venture, by taking a chance on someone, or by opening yourself up to a new experience, you are opening yourself up to potential hurt. *Risk has almost a 100% guarantee you'll get hurt in the long run.* But life is about risk, isn't it?

There's that cliché phrase: No risk, no reward. But that cliché is truth. Life is worth taking a chance on. People are worth taking a chance on. When you get hurt, I'll be here, and I'll have an extra bag of chips and salsa for us to commiserate over. But when things turn out unimaginably better than you could have hoped? I'll be there, too. With high fives, and a "*see, I knew you could do it!*" And hell, we'll celebrate with not only chips and salsa, but with queso, baby. You. Deserve. Queso.

REFLECTION: *May I choose to take some risks in life, even when I know it might not turn out the way I hope. May I understand that hurt and learning teaches me as much about myself as winning and reward. May I be humble and grateful in both.*

NOTES ON HOPE

You been here before? End of your rope and holding desperately onto hope? This is for you.

Hey babe. I want you to listen to me. Eyes up, babe, right here. Look at me. Things look unimaginably dark right now, I know they do. You have no strength left. Your body is battered and covered in dirt and sadness, and you have been bruised and bloodied by the world. Life has not been kind, I know. Or rather, some parts of life have not only been *unkind*, they've been unimaginably cruel. You carry the weight of a deep and torturous suffering like a backpack filled with boulders. Every physical piece of you hurts. Your skin has the scars of a thousand paper cuts of viciousness and most of all, your heart feels deep and inexpressible pain. It is knotted and twisted in agony, the hurt reaching a depth you didn't know existed.

Honey, I know. Things look about as hopeless as they can be, and all you have left is a hail Mary and a "screw it, what have I got to lose?" And maybe you believe in your heart that you don't have even one damn thing left to lose. This is it. It's all you've got. Nothing left.

But I promise you, there is so, so much you have that is worthy of good, so much that is worthy of the promise of a future.

YOU HAVE EVERYTHING YOU NEED INSIDE OF YOU.

Because even if you feel like you've lost nearly everything, you still have a glimmer, a grain, a speck of this one thing that can't be denied. It is clawing its way out of the center of your soul, gasping for air and trying desperately to reach the surface.

That thing is Hope.

Hope is the thing that keeps you begrudgingly dragging one foot alongside of the other, even if your head is hung, shuffling your heavy legs stubbornly across the scarred and dusty ground. Hope is the thing that compels you to take one more breath into your lungs when your chest is so weak you can't possibly take anything more in. It's unbearable. There's no way you can do it. But somehow, you do. Hope is the thing that keeps you *trying*. Endlessly, stubbornly trying, even when you've tried every fucking thing there is to try and there can't possibly be anything else you could attempt. Right? Could there be?

When there is *one more try*, even though you think you've covered the vast ground of everything, that *try* is a quiet longing to keep going. *Hope is a desperate, pale glow, a weak but flickering ember at the center of your soul.* Hope isn't shiny or bold. It isn't vibrant or sexy and it's not often fun. But it's there, undeniable in its very existence.

I see you, and I see hope *in* you. I know you. I *am* you. Baby girl, I know you've been bracing yourself against the storm for so long that bracing yourself has become the only thing holding you up. Your legs are collapsing under the weight of your own being. But still, you go on. Nevertheless, you hope.

I met Monique when I was speaking once in St. Louis and she told me that during a particularly brutal time in her family's life, her brother said to her on the phone, "Yeah, but hope dies last." It resonated, and it was her first tattoo. "Hope Dies Last." I've read books and studied habits and searched for bright spots and silver linings in a thousand clouds, and I'd never heard it stated so beautifully, so simply.

Hope dies last.

After everything else is gone, after everything you've tried, one more try means there is hope. Hope doesn't die after you've tried a thousand times. It doesn't even die after you've tried one thousand and thirteen times. *Hope is infinite tries.* Hope is the next breath, the next step, the answer to the next question when you refuse to stop asking the questions. Even if the only question you can ask is simply to whisper, "Why?" Even if the only words you can shallowly breathe are, "I can't."

You can. Babe, you look me in the eyes. You listen to me. Don't give up. Don't quit. I know it hurts. I know you think you can't go on. Keep going. Keep moving forward, even if progress is measured in centimeters instead of miles. Keep moving.

Hope is in you because you are still alive and sometimes staying alive is the bravest thing you can do. Hope is not dead, because you are not. Because hope dies last.

REFLECTION: *May I remember that, even when I think all is gone and all is lost, there is one thing left: Hope. May I cling to hope like a life preserve when I am desperate, even if that life preserve is unimaginably small. May I see it for what it is: a true life saver. Because hope dies last.*

EPILOGUE
Messy Missy

My family used to call me Messy Missy. It was meant as an affectionate term, and one that was certainly fitting. My wispy blonde hair was windblown and tangled and falling in front of my face. I was pudgy and round, I wore my brother's hand-me-down plaid bell bottoms, and I perpetually had chocolate ice cream or some other dirt or food all over my cheeks. Sometimes it was used more affectionately than others, as a relative once rolled her eyes and cried with exasperation, "Oh Missy, you are *such* a basket case." If I'm being honest, I've been trying to outrun and outright bury Messy Missy my whole life.

I've spent decades attempting to prove I'm not a basket case, years demonstrating I am everything that Messy Missy was not. I've spent hundreds of hours and a small fortune in hair salons, nail salons, lash salons, and tanning salons chasing the perfect look and glowing skin.

I've carefully studied how professional people speak and I've not only taken notes, but also adopted their very syntax and voice inflection. When I've heard someone use a word that made them sound wise, I've tucked that word away and adopted it into my own vocabulary.

I've done my best to dress well, be on top of the chaos, and be a part of the right social circles. I have coffee dates with the "right" people. Not everything is strategic, I really like a vast majority of the people in those groups. But I sure do love being a part of the important people and organizations in my community. I wrote in a journal once: the thing that would surprise younger me about present day me is that I'm actually one of the popular girls now. Popular is a goofy term, but it's a great illustration of how I've come such a long way from there to here. It is astonishing, especially to me.

I've worked together with a team, and we've built a business that always has a shine and polish on it, even on days when I feel like I'm dying inside. I've coached and developed and led leaders because I want to help them grow into their own talents and power. I live in a nice neighborhood and drive a nice car and my kitchen counters are clean and I go to the dentist every six months, and I make my bed every morning. Ok fine, not every morning, but most of them. Messy Missy may have been a basket case, but present day me looks like she has her shit together

But the thing about Messy Missy is that I've never been able to outrun her. Wherever I go, she's with me. I've never been able to bury her because even when I'm striving so hard to perfect all the things, she's reminding me that my messiness isn't on the outside, it's inside, and no matter how I try to perfect my public-facing world, my inner world is the one that deserves the most attention. I can't outrun her. I'm also learning that I don't need to outrun her or bury her or silence her. *I just need to love her.*

I'm learning that she needs me to kneel in front of her, gently brush the wispy hair out of her eyes, kiss her softly on the cheek, and tell her she is perfect exactly the way she is. She's perfect with chocolate ice cream on her cheek and dirt under her fingernails. She's perfect when her hair is done and when it's undone. She's perfect when her bed is made and when the covers are thrown haphazardly to the side.

SHE IS INDEED MESSY, AND SHE IS PERFECT, AND SHE IS LOVED.

I'm having more conversations with her than I ever have before. When she tells me she's tired and needs a nap, I've stopped telling her she's lazy and instead I've said, "Ok honey, let's lay down for a few minutes." When she tells me she's anxious and overwhelmed because we've been around people all week and had to be "on" for everyone and she needs some time alone, I've started to give her the time and space she needs to reclaim her peace. She has always worried that each opportunity might be the last one that comes her way and has felt like she had to desperately grab onto every single one. Now, I'm working to remind her that opportunities come and go, and we can trust that there will always be more.

I'm learning that fifteen or even twenty pounds overweight doesn't define her. Neither does forty pounds overweight. Neither does ten pounds underweight. The number on the scale doesn't matter so much as the weight of the care and love in her heart. Fancy bathroom scales measure a lot of things, but they don't calculate a person's authenticity or the quality of their heart.

So, if Messy Missy and I could leave you with anything, we would tell you to say kind words to others, but save the most gentle and encouraging ones for yourself. We would tell you to let yourself rest when you're tired. We would tell you to eat the damn cheesecake when you want it. We'd hope against hope that we've left you with a deep and profound knowing that you are enough, and an understanding that there is nothing you can do, or say, or strive for, or be that makes you any more loveable than you already are. Or anything you can do that makes you less loveable. You. Are. Enough. Just like that. Because you're here, and because you are, you are so enough, there aren't even enough "enoughs" to tell you how enough you already are. Please take that all the way into your bones, feel it, and believe it.

I don't know where to end except for exactly as I began, by saying two words: Thank you. Those words really are the beginning and the end of this book, with everything else sandwiched in between. I don't know if this book is a love letter to my daughters, to you, to myself, or to every single one of us, but I know it was written over time and space and with the utmost tenderness and care. This book helped me brave the terrain of places I didn't even know were still inside of me and helped me gently lay down some heavy things I hadn't realized I'd still been carrying. Writing this book has helped me dig into places I had been afraid to go. That's what writing does: it helps us unearth what's beneath the surface, just waiting to be discovered. Sometimes we find gems, and sometimes we come across sharp and ugly rocks. Both of these are equally important and deeply meaningful discoveries and believe it or not, both are treasures. I'm overcome with immense gratitude that you took the time to dig a little deeper, further, longer with me. The treasure of breakthrough is worth the effort. Let's keep digging.

WITH BLESSINGS AND GRATITUDE,

MELISSA
11-4-22

ACKNOWLEDGEMENTS

Dearest Reader, your time is a gift, one which I will never take for granted. Like everything in my life, my simple hope is that I've left you better than I found you. To my children, I have no words that will adequately convey my deep and covering love for each of you. The joy you bring to my life is inexpressible and my admiration as I watch each of you grow into your own brand of adult is a magic I didn't know existed. I am so proud of you. I can say that because I know *you* are all proud of you, too. I said it before and I'll say it again: In all of my lifetime, my greatest legacy is you. To Amanda, for your practical and sacrificial heart. You are my confidant and my person and the greatest travel partner, and I am endlessly indebted for everything you do and for everything you are. I'm still not a fan of "Feldy math," but I appreciate it. To my parents, for acting like I hung the moon. When you say you're amazed by me, I want you to know that even when I laugh it off, I hear you and I tuck those words into my heart for those days when I don't feel so amazing. To my precious and loved Oh My Cupcakes! team: Though many have come and gone, and the shape of the team has evolved over time, each of you has left an indelible fingerprint on both the business and my heart. My heart swells when I watch you all grow with or without me being in the shops. I don't know what God has next, but I'm glad to be on the ride with you. To "Ganel and Max," Ella and Beckett, thank you for making our family a part of your family. There were never better neighbors or "framily." I'll cook tonight, just bring the kids over before basketball. Unless Max is frying fish, then we'll be right over. To JoJo and Nate, my fondness for live music grows exponentially by the day, as does my deep admiration for you two. Love you dudes. Let's hit up a concert soon.

The list is long and I know I'll forget someone and kick myself later, but to Shelli, thank you for being in my corner and showing me what I'm capable of. To Pat, thank you for reminding me that it's ok to say no sometimes, even to "really good opportunities." To coaches Pam and Jen, you taught me confidence in leadership like never before, which has allowed me the courage to step away from some things and the faith to step into others. To those who kept asking me, "is your book done yet?" I offer humble gratitude. Danel, Jayne, MarShondria, Mak, Sheri, you were never nagging me. Quite the opposite, I felt compelled to keep going because even when I would have given up on myself, I couldn't let you down. To the women who have entrusted me with their writing journey during writing retreats and workshops I've hosted, your encouragement and belief made me believe in myself, too. Nichelle, Angela, April, Sarah, Jeni, Jeanette, Megan, and Kristi, I will never forget those autumn days in Nebraska. *"What happened in those woods," they asked. "Magic," she said.* Indeed, it was. That's what happened within these pages, too: magic was created. The magic was intended for you, but I felt it sprinkle and pour all over me.

And as an arc over everything I do, every blessing I have, and every talent I've been given, and every grace I never deserved, I offer thanks to God. What an incredible, blessed life I get to lead. Wow. Just wow. This is cool.

APPENDIX

LIST OF VALUES

Accountability
Adaptability
Authenticity
Autonomy
Awareness
Balance
Belief
Capability
Care
Challenge
Collaboration
Commitment
Community
Compassion
Connection
Consistency
Creativity
Dedication
Dependability
Development
Discipline
Diversity
Efficiency
Empathy
Empowerment
Encouragement
Engagement
Enthusiasm
Equality
Ethics
Excellence
Excitement
Faith
Family
Flexibility
Freedom
Friendliness
Fun
Generosity
Goodness
Gratitude
Growth
Hard work
Honesty
Honor
Hope
Humanity
Humility
Inclusivity
Independence
Individuality
Influence
Innovation
Integrity
Intellect
Judiciousness
Justice
Leadership
Learning
Love
Loyalty
Motivation
Open-mindedness
Opportunity
Optimism
Order
Passion
Philanthropy
Playfulness
Positivity
Pragmatism
Privacy
Professionalism
Prosperity
Purpose
Recognition
Relating to others
Relaxation
Reliability
Respect
Responsibility
Satisfaction
Security
Self-Care
Sensitivity
Serving Others
Significance
Spirituality
Stability
Status
Stewardship
Strength
Teamwork
Transparency
Trust
Trustworthiness
Truth
Value
Virtue
Wellness

MELISSA M. JOHNSON

Melissa J Creative

Melissa sees possibility and potential in people even before they believe in themselves. Melissa is the founder and CEO of Oh My Cupcakes!, Sweet Cream Candle Co., and Melissa J. Creative. Her businesses are built with intention to create beautiful things that bring people joy.

With a background in broadcast media and communications, Melissa is a sought-after keynote speaker with both Melissa J Creative and the Jon Gordon Companies, where she is a Power of Positive Leadership Certified speaker and trainer. Melissa finds purpose in helping people discover and engage their own greatest gifts and has a mission to spread the message of empowerment or growth with a positive mindset. Melissa delivers dynamic and electrifying keynotes and trainings as well as writing workshops and retreats. She engages her audiences with personal stories, a twist of wit, and a warm, approachable spirit that moves people to their own lightbulb moments of understanding. She is frequently invited to appear on panels presenting on: building phenomenal company cultures, women's business ownership, positive leadership, and adopting and parenting children who come from hard places.

People have said Melissa "just has a presence about her." Her genuine desire is to inspire and uplift, leaving people better than she found them. Melissa's first book, Fingers in the Frosting: God's Hand on the Creation of Oh My Cupcakes! is available where books are sold.

Melissa was born and raised in the heart of the Midwest and is a blessed mother to four children, three dogs, and one disagreeable cat.